A BIBLIOGRAPHY OF ELECTRONIC MUSIC

A BIBLIOGRAPHY
OF ELECTRONIC
||||| MUSIC |||||

37485

Compiled by

LOWELL M. CROSS

University of Toronto Press

to

my wife

Nora

PREFACE

The following compilation of writings on electronic music was undertaken as a graduate research project at the University of Toronto in the autumn of 1964, following a suggestion by the late Dr. Myron Schaeffer, one of the founders of the university's Electronic Music Studio. A modest beginning was made during the preceding year at Texas Technological College in collaboration with Professor Charles Lawrie, the first of the author's teachers to encourage his interest in electronic music.

Dr. Schaeffer proposed that an expanded bibliography would supply the sources for a graduate essay on the early developments in electronic music between 1948 and 1953 as well as provide a useful reference for all persons associated with the Electronic Music Studio. After Dr. Schaeffer's death in January, 1965, the supervision of the thesis and the bibliography passed to Professor Gustav Ciamaga, who succeeded Dr. Schaeffer as director of the studio.

The books, articles, monographs, and abstracts cited here represent an attempt to compile as exhaustive a bibliography as possible for "musique concrète," "elektronische Musik," "tape music," "computer music," and the closely related fields in experimental music. Access to the extensive holdings of the Electronic Music Studio and the libraries of the University of Toronto has permitted the verification of a large number of entries by individual inspection. However, since an attempt to examine each item listed here for purposes of authentication, annotation, or classification would have greatly exceeded the scope of the project, a degree of reliance upon secondary sources was necessary. In addition to the bibliographies of Austin, Basart, Berlind, Deliège, Henry, Martin, and Répertoire International des Musiques Expérimentales, the sources consulted most frequently were the periodical indexes, including The Music Index, Reader's Guide to Periodical Literature, and the indexes to the Journal of the Acoustical Society of America.

The innovative and controversial developments in this rapidly expanding field have produced a body of

literature that ranges from highly technical works to
writings of a generalized, popular, and often sensation-
seeking nature. It was for this reason that an alpha-
betical rather than a classified arrangement of the cita-
tions was chosen. An index has been provided to aid in
the location of some of the more significant items.

I wish to acknowledge my indebtedness not only to
Professors Schaeffer, Lawrie, and Ciamaga, but also to
my colleagues at the University of Toronto who offered
their assistance during the past academic year. The
contributions of Mr. Anthony J. Gnazzo and Professor
Harvey J. Olnick have been especially valuable.

Lowell M. Cross

Toronto
November, 1966

The second printing incorporates a number of cor-
rections and revisions. I am very grateful to Mr. Hugh
Davies, London, for his many helpful suggestions.

L.M.C.

Toronto
June, 1968

CONTENTS

Preface   vii

A Bibliography of Electronic Music   1

Index   123

A BIBLIOGRAPHY OF ELECTRONIC MUSIC

1. Aare, Leif. "Funderingar kring det radikala." Musi-
   kern, 3 (March 1964), 10.

2. Abbiati, Franco. "Libera musica e musica di stato."
   La Scala, 127 (June 1960), 7.

3. "Activities in the field of electronic music." World
   of Music, 2 (Oct. 1957), 7.

4. Adam, Max. "Der Tonmeister: eine neue Berufsmöglich-
   keit für den Musiker." Schweizerische Musikzeitung, C, 1 (1960), 35.

5. Adams, Karl Heinz. "Filter circuits for electronic
   sound production." Ottawa, National Research Council of Canada, Technical Translation TT-605, 1956
   (translation of 6).

6. ------ "Siebschaltungen als elektrische Klangmittel."
   Technische Hausmitteilungen des Nordwestdeutschen
   Rundfunks, VI, 1-2 (1954), 18.

7. Adelsic, M. Svet zvoka in glasbe. Ljubljana, 1964.

8. ------ Svet zvoka in glasbe. Reviewed in Zvuk, 64
   (1965), 507.

9. Adorno, Theodor W. Der getreue Korrepetitor. Frankfurt, Fischer Verlag, 1963.

10. ------ Der getreue Korrepetitor. Reviewed in Schwei-
    zerische Musikzeitung, CIII, 4 (1963), 239.

11. ------ "Invecchiamento della musica nuovo." La Ras-
    segna musicale, XXVIII, 1 (March 1957), 1.

12. ------ "Kritieren -- Extrait de l'introduction à une
    cycle de conférences." Darmstädter Beiträge zur
    neuen Musik, I (1958).

13. ------ "Modern music is growing old." Score, 18 (Dec. 1956), 18 (translated by Rollo H. Myers).

14. ------ "Zum Verhältnis von Musik und Technik heute"/ "Technique, technology, and music to-day." Gravesaner Blätter/Gravesano Review, III, 11-12 (1958), 36/51.

15. Albersheim, Gerhard L. "Mind and matter in music." Journal of Aesthetics and Art Criticism, XXII, 3 (1964), 289.

16. Albrecht, G. Letter. Scientific American, CXCIV, 4 (1956), 18.

17. Albrecht, Jan. "K estetike dodekafonie a elektronickej hudby." Slovenská Hudba, III, 2 (Jan. 1959), 11.

18. Aldous, D.W. "London newsletter." High Fidelity, II (Nov.-Dec., 1952), 47; IV, (August 1954), 38.

19. Amenabar, J. See Asuar, José Vicente.

20. "Amsterdam: Seriële schilderijen en elektronische Musiek." Mens en Melodie, XVII (June 1962), 187.

21. Amy, Gilbert. "Orchestre et espace sonore." Esprit, XXVIII, 280 (Jan. 1960), 75.

22. ------ "Sur quelques problèmes récents et ... futurs." Phantomas, 15-16 (Jan. 1960).

23. Andersen, Mogens. "'Klangfarbenmelodie' i orgelmusik." Dansk Musiktidsskrift, XXXIV (Nov. 1959), 233.

24. Anderson, Owen. "New York (Second Annual New York Festival of the Avant-Garde)." Music Journal, XXII, 8 (Nov. 1964), 72.

25. Ando, Yoshinoir. See Takatsuji, Tsukasa.

26. Anfilov, Gleb. Fisika i muzyka. Moskva, Mir, 1964. Translated as Physics and music. Moskva, Mir, 1966.

27. Ansermet, Ernest. "The crisis of contemporary music." Recorded Sound, 13 (Jan. 1964), 165.

28. "ANS -- nowy instrument elektronowy." Ruch Muzyczny, VI, 5 (1962), 23.

29. Anthologies de la musique concrète (recordings). Reviewed in Disques, 80 (August-Sept. 1956), 488.

30. Appleton, Jon. "Aesthetic direction in electronic music." Western Humanities Review, XVIII, 4 (Autumn 1964), 345.

31. ------ "Report from Yale: festival of contemporary American music." Current Musicology, (Spring 1966), 65.

32. ------ "Tone-relation, time displacement and timbre: an approach to twentieth-century music." The Music Review, XXVIII, 1 (Feb. 1966), 54.

33. Arnheim, Rudolf. "Information theory, an introductory note." Journal of Aesthetics and Art Criticism, XVII, 4 (June 1959), 501.

34. "The art of telharmony." Electrical World, XLVII, 10 (March 10, 1906), 509.

35. Arthuys, Philippe. "La pensée et l'instrument." La Revue musicale, 236 (1957), 128.

36. ------ "Pour commencer." La Revue musicale, 236 (1957), 8.

37. ------ "Première décade internationale de musique expérimentale." Cahiers d'information musicale du CDMI, 9-10 (Summer-Autumn 1953), 30.

38. Aschoff, Volker. "Elektro-akustik und Musik." Beiträge zur Musikgeschichte der Stadt Aachen, 37.

39. Asuar, José Vicente. "En el umbral de una nueva era musical." Revista Musical Chilena, XIII, 64 (March-April 1959), 11.

40. ------ "Música electrónica: poética musical de nues-

tros dias." <u>Revista Musical Chilena</u>, XVII, 86 (1963), 12.

41. ------ "Y ... sigamos componiendo: sobre metodologia." <u>Revista Musical Chilena</u>, XVII, 83 (Jan.-March (1963), 55.

42. ------ and J. Amenabar. "Montaje de un laboratorio electrónico musical." <u>Revista Musical Chilena</u>, XII (July-August 1958), 150.

43. "Atombomben Musik." <u>Hausmusik</u>, XXI (March-April 1957), 55.

44. Attneave, Fred. "Stochastic compositional processes." <u>Journal of Aesthetics and Art Criticism</u>, XVII, 4 (June 1959), 503.

45. Auer-Sedak, E. "Funkcionalnost moderne muzike." <u>Zvuk</u>, 55 (1962), 519.

46. Austin, William W. <u>Music in the 20th century</u>. New York, W.W. Norton, 1966, 374, 377, 431, 652.

47. "Automation in music." <u>Music and Musicians</u>, IX (Feb. 1961), 21.

48. Babbitt, Milton. "Compositional techniques and electronic media" (abstract). <u>Journal of the Acoustical Society of America</u>, XXIX (1957), 770.

49. ------ "Electronic music: the revolution in sound." <u>University, A Princeton Magazine</u>, 4 (Spring, 1960).

50. ------ "An introduction." <u>Journal of Music Theory</u>, VII, 1 (1963), vi.

51. ------ "An introduction to the R.C.A. Synthesizer." <u>Journal of Music Theory</u>, VIII, 2 (1964), 251.

52. ------ "Past and present concepts of the nature and limits of music." <u>Report of the Eighth Congress of the International Musicological Society, New York, 1961</u>. Kassel, Bärenreiter Verlag, 1961, Volume I, 398.

53. ------ "The revolution in sound: electronic music."
    Music Journal, XVIII, 7 (Oct. 1960), 34.

54. ------ "The synthesis, perception, and specification
    of musical time." Journal of the International
    Folk Music Council, XVI (1964), 92.

55. ------ "Twelve-tone rhythmic structure and the elec-
    tronic medium." Perspectives of New Music, I, 1
    (Fall 1962), 49.

56. ------ "Who cares if you listen?" High Fidelity,
    VIII, 2 (Feb. 1958), 38.

57. Bachmann, Claus Henning. "Die Musik im Zeitalter der
    Technik." Begegnung, X (1955), 261. Kulturarbeit,
    VII (1955), 183.

58. Backus, John. "Die Reihe: a scientific evaluation."
    Perspectives of New Music, I, 1 (Fall 1962), 160.

59. Badings, Henk. "Electronic music: its development in
    the Netherlands." Delta, I (Winter 1958-59), 85.

60. ------ "Experiences with electronic ballet music."
    In Beckwith and Kasemets, eds., The modern compo-
    ser and his world. Toronto, University of Toronto
    Press, 1961, 106.

61. ------ "Sur les possibilites et les limitations de
    la musique électronique." Revue Belge de Musico-
    logie, XIII, 1-4 (1959), 57.

62. ------ and J.W. de Bruyn. "Electronic music."
    Philips Technical Review, XIX (Dec. 23, 1957), 191;
    (Jan. 30, 1958), 201. Annales des Télécommunica-
    tions, 102876 (April, 1958).

63. Baker, Ray Stannard. "New music for an old world."
    McClure's Magazine, XXVII, 3 (July 1906), 291.

64. Baker, Robert A. "Musicomp -- music-simulator for
    compositional procedures for the IBM 7090
    electronic digital computer." Urbana, University
    of Illinois Experimental Music Studio, Technical
    Report No. 9, 1962 (mimeograph).

65. ------ "Preparation of Musicwriter punched paper tape for use by the Illiac electronic digital computer." Urbana, University of Illinois Experimental Music Studio, Technical Report No. 2, June, 1961 (mimeograph).

66. ------ See Hiller, Lejaren A., Jr.

67. "Ballet score by Remi Gassman." American Musician, (March 1961), 14.

68. Band, Lothar. "Das elektrische Musikinstrument: sein Wert und seine Grenzen." Musikwoche, XIV (1954), 35.

69. Barbaud, Pierre. "Avènement de la musique cybernetique." Les Lettres nouvelles, VII, 8 (April 22, 1959), 28.

70. ------ Initiation à la composition musicale automatique. Paris, Dunod, 1965.

71. ------ "Musique algorithmique." Esprit, XXVIII, 280 (Jan. 1960), 92. Bulletin Technique de la Compagnie des Machines Bull, 2 (1961), 22.

72. Barbour, J. Murray. Letter (comment on Olson and Belar, "Aid to music ... "). Journal of the Acoustical Society of America, XXXIV (1962), 128.

73. ------ "Music and electricity." Papers, American Musicological Society, (Dec. 29-30, 1937), 3.

74. Barraud, Henri. "Musique concrète." Musical America, LXXIII (Jan. 15, 1953), 6.

75. Barron, Louis and Bebe. "Forbidden planet." Film Music, XV (Summer 1956), 18.

76. Baruch, Gerth-Wolfgang. "Was ist Musique concrète?" Melos, XX (Jan. 1953), 9.

77. Basart, Ann Phillips. Serial music: a classified bibliography of writings on twelve-tone and electronic music. Berkeley and Los Angeles, University of California Press, 1961.

78. ------ Serial music. Reviewed in Music Magazine,
    CLSIV (Feb. 1962), 51.

79. ------ Serial music. Reviewed in Music Review,
    XXIII (1962), 155.

80. ------ Serial music. Reviewed in The Musical Times,
    CIII (March 1962), 177.

81. ------ Serial music. Reviewed in Musikforschung,
    XVII, 3 (1964), 318.

82. ------ Serial music. Reviewed in Notes, XIX, 2 (1962),
    256.

83. ------ Serial music. Reviewed in Svensk Tidskrift
    för Musikforskning, XLIV (1962), 73.

84. Beauchamp, James W. "The harmonic tone generator, a
    voltage-controlled device for additive synthesis
    of audio harmonic spectra." Audio Engineering
    Society Preprint No. 323, Oct. 1964.

85. ------ "A report on the Magnavox sponsored research
    investigation 'the development of new electronic
    systems for generating musical sound.'" Urbana,
    University of Illinois Experimental Music Studio,
    Technical Report No. 10, August 1964 (mimeograph).

86. ------ "A statement of progress on the research in-
    vestigation 'generation and creation of new elec-
    tronic sounds.'" Urbana, University of Illinois
    Experimental Studio, Technical Report No. 7, August
    1963 (mimeograph).

87. ------ See Hiller, Lejaren A., Jr.

88. Becerra, Gustavo. "Que es la música electrónica?"
    Revista Musical Chilena, XI (Dec. 1957), 27.

89. Beckwith, John. "Notes on some new music heard on
    CBC radio." Canadian Music Journal, IV, 2 (Winter
    1960), 37.

90. ------ and Udo Kasemets, eds. The modern composer
    and his world. Toronto, University of Toronto

Press, 1961.

91. Beeson, Jack. "Otto Luening." <u>Bulletin of American Composers Alliance</u>, III, 3 (Autumn 1953), 2.

92. Behrman, David. "The changing landscape of contemporary music." <u>Selmer Bandwagon</u>, XIII, 5 (Nov. 1965), 16.

93. "Béjarts Triumph in Köln." <u>Melos</u>, XXIX (July-August 1962), 244.

94. Belar, Herbert. See Olson, Harry F.

95. Bellac, P. "Der Stereophoner A"/"The stereophoner A." <u>Gravesaner Blätter/Gravesano Review</u>, III, 11-12 (1958), 123/124.

96. Benary, P. "Raum und Zeit in heutigen musikalischen Denken." <u>Schweizerische Musikzeitung</u>, CIV, 6 (1964) 338.

97. Bender, William. "Electronic music." <u>Electronic Age</u>, (Spring 1965), 10.

98. Bentzon, Johan. "Lydkunst somfag ved konservatoriet." <u>Dansk Musiktidsskrift</u>, XXXV (April 1960), 131.

99. ------ "Svigtende spilleglaede." <u>Dansk Musiktidsskrift</u>, XXXVIII, 2 (1963), 62.

100. Berger, Arthur. "Music written for tape recording." <u>Bulletin of American Composers Alliance</u>, II, 4 (1952-53), 17.

101. Berio, Luciano. "Musik und Dichtung: eine Erfahrung." <u>Darmstädter Beiträge zur neuen Musik</u>, 2 (1959), 36.

102. ------ "Note sull musica elettronica." <u>Ricordiana</u>, III (Oct. 1957), 427.

103. ------ "Poésie et musique: une expérience." <u>Revue Belge de Musicologie</u>, XIII, 1-4 (1959), 68.

104. ------ "Prospettive nella musica, richerche ed attività dello studio di fonologia musicale di radio

Milano." _Elettronica_, V, 3 (Sept. 1956), 108.

105. ------ "The studio di fonologia musicale of the Milan
     radio." _Score_, 15 (March 1956), 83.

106. ------ "Sur la musique électronique." _Schweizerische_
     Musikzeitung, XCVII (June 1957), 233.

107. Berk, Ernest. "My philosophy of musique concrète."
     International Sound Engineer, II, 2 (Jan. 1964), 42.

108. Berlincioni, A. "Mathematic-acoustic principles of
     the electric composition of sounds." _Audiotecnica_,
     I, II, III (1965), 9.

109. Berlind, Gary. "Writings on the use of computers in
     music." New York, New York University Institute
     for Computer Research in the Humanities, 1965 (mim-
     eograph).

110. Bernheimer, M. "Stockhausen's non-lecture." _Satur-_
     day Review, XLVII (Jan. 25, 1964), 44.

111. Berridge, J.W. "The Hamograph, a new approach to
     electronic music." _Audio_, XLVI (Oct. 1962), 23.

112. Beyer, Robert. "Elektronische Musik." _Melos_, XXI
     (1954), 35.

113. ------ "Die Klangwelt der elektronischen Musik."
     Zeitschrift für Musik, CXIII (Feb. 1952), 74.

114. ------ "Das Problem der 'kommenden Musik.'" _Die_
     Musik, XX, 12 (Sept. 1928), 861.

115. ------ "Zur Geschichte der elektronischen Musik."
     Melos, XX (1953), 278.

116. ------ "Zur Situation der elektronischen Musik."
     Zeitschrift für Musik, CXVI (August-Sept. 1955),
     452.

117. Bied, Alphonse. "Robots compositeurs de musique."
     Technica, (Nov. 1955).

118. Bierl, R. "Das Problem der Schwingungserzeugung aus

der neueren Musikinstrumentenforschung und Entwicklung." Frequenz, XIII, 8 (1959), 250. Annales
des Télécommunications, 123258 (Jan. 1960).

119. ------ "Neuere Ergebnisse der Elektrischen Klangerzeugung und deren Beziehungen zu des Mechanischen
Klangerzeugung." Acustica, IV, 1 (1954), 218.

120. "Bill to copyright new electronic sounds offered."
Billboard, LXXI, (March 16, 1959), 1.

121. Blacher, Boris. "Die musikalische Komposition unter
dem Einfluss der technischen Entwicklung der Musik."
In Winckel, ed., Klangstruktur der Musik. Berlin,
Verlag für Radio-Foto-Kinotechnik, 1955, 203.

122. Blaukopf, Kurt. "Balzac im elektronischen Studio."
Oesterreichische Musikzeitschrift, XII (April
1957), 154.

123. ------ Hexenküche der Musik. Teufen/St. Gallen,
A. Niggli, 1956.

124. ------ Hexenküche der Musik. Reviewed in Mens en
Melodie, XII (Nov. 1957), 358.

125. ------ Hexenküche der Musik. Reviewed in Musica,
XI (March 1957), 180.

126. ------ Hexenküche der Musik. Reviewed in Neue Zeitschrift für Musik, CXVIII (Nov. 1957), 648.

127. ------ Hexenküche der Musik. Reviewed in Oesterreichische Musikzeitschrift, XII (March 1957),
127.

128. Blomdahl, Karl-Birger. "Aniara." In Beckwith and
Kasemets, eds., The modern composer and his world.
Toronto, University of Toronto Press, 1961, 102.

129. Blume, Friedrich, et al. "Was ist Musik?" Melos,
XXVI (March 1959), 65.

130. Bode, Harald. "Audio-system synthesizer." In
McGraw-Hill Yearbook of Science and Technology.
New York, McGraw-Hill, 1963, 133.

131. ------ "Die elektrischen Musikinstrumente." <u>Das Elektron</u>, III, 5 (1949), 193.

132. ------ "European electronic music instrument design." <u>Journal of the Audio Engineering Society</u>, IX, 4 (Oct. 1961), 267.

133. ------ Letter ("Regarding the integrated electronic music console of the University of Illinois"). <u>Journal of the Audio Engineering Society</u>, XIII, 4 (Oct. 1965), 360 (with reply from L.A. Hiller, Jr.).

134. ------ "Mehrstimmige und vollstimmige elektrische Musikinstrumente." <u>Das Elektron</u>, III, 6 (1949), 211.

135. ------ "Das Melochord des Studios für elektronische Musik im Funkhaus Köln." <u>Technische Hausmitteilungen des Nordwestdeutschen Rundfunks</u>, VI, 1-2 (1954), 27.

136. ------ "The Melochord of the Cologne Studio for Electronic Music." Ottawa, National Research Council of Canada, Technical Translation TT-607, 1956 (Translation of 135).

137. ------ "New tool for the exploration of unknown electronic music instrument performances." <u>Journal of the Audio Engineering Society</u>, IX, 4 (Oct. 1961), 261.

138. ------ "New tool for the exploration of unknown sound resources for composers" (abstract). <u>Journal of the Acoustical Society of America</u>, XXXIII (1961), 861.

139. ------ "Solid-state audio frequency spectrum shifter." Audio Engineering Society Preprint No. 395, 1965.

140. ------ "Sound synthesizer creates new musical effects." <u>Electronics</u>, XXXIV (Dec. 1, 1961), 33.

141. Bodnar, J. "Clovek v pretechnizovanom svete." <u>Slovenská Hudba</u>, VIII, 4 (1964), 97.

142. Boehm, Laszlo. <u>Modern music notation</u>. New York,

G. Schirmer, 1961.

143. Bokesova, Z. "K otazke experimentu." _Slovenská_
Hudba, V (Nov. 1961), 468.

144. Boretz, Benjamin. "Music." _The Nation_, CXCVI (March
16, 1963), 233.

145. Borko, Harold, ed. _Computer applications in the_
behavioral sciences. Englewood Cliffs, N.J.,
Prentice-Hall, 1962.

146. Borneman, E. "One-night stand (electronic computing
machine)." _Melody Maker_, XXVIII (Nov. 29, 1952),
5.

147. Bornoff, Jack. "Friedrich Trautwein (zum Gedächt-
nis)." _Gravesaner Blätter_, 7-8 (April 1957), 3.

148. Bose, Fritz. "Elektronik und Hausmusik." _Musica_,
IX (1955), 115.

149. "Boston: Bethany Beardslee singing to Milton Babbitt's
music." _Musical Courier_, CLXIII, 12 (Nov. 1961),
60.

150. Bottje, Will Gay. "Electronic music." _The Instru-_
mentalist, XVIII (May 1964), 52.

151. Boucourechliev, André. "La fin et les moyens." _La_
Revue musicale, 244 (1959), 30.

152. ------ "La musique électronique." _Esprit_, XXVIII,
280 (Jan. 1960), 98.

153. ------ "Problèmes de la musique moderne." _La Nou-_
velle revue française, VII (Dec. 1959-Jan. 1960).

154. Boulez, Pierre. "À la limite du pays fertile." In
Relevés d'apprenti. Paris, Éditions du Seuil, 1966.
"An der Grenze des Fruchtlandes"/"At the ends of
fruitful land." _Die Reihe_, I/1 (1955/1958), 47/19.

155. ------ "Communication." In Pierre Schaeffer, "Concrète (musique)." _Encyclopédie de la musique._
Paris, Fasquelle, 1958, 577.

156. ------ "Son, verb, synthèse." <u>Melos</u>, XXV (Oct. 1958), 310. <u>Revue Belge de Musicologie</u>, XIII, (1959), 5.

157. ------ "Tendances de la musique récente." <u>La Revue musicale</u>, 236 (1957), 28.

158. Bowers, Faubion. "Electronics as music." <u>Saturday Review</u>, XLIV, 45 (Nov. 11, 1961), 60.

159. Bowsher, John M. See Le Caine, Hugh.

160. Brautigam, E. "Musikalische Städtebilder." <u>Musica</u>, XV, 5-6 (May-June 1961), 310.

161. Brennecke, Wilfried. "Musizieren leicht gemacht." <u>Musica</u>, IX (1955), 158.

162. Bress, Hyman. "The role of electronic music in relationship to the violin." <u>Musical Events</u>, XVII (April 1962), 8.

163. Breuer, Robert. "Die Avantgarde in den Vereinigten Staaten." <u>Melos</u>, XXX, 3 (March 1963), 77.

164. ------ "Die Avantgarde wirbelt viel Staub in New York auf." <u>Melos</u>, XXXI, 3 (March 1964), 103.

165. ------ "A new dimension in music." <u>Showcase</u>, XL, 5 (1961), 8.

166. Briner, Ermanno. "Das Tonmeisterproblem." <u>Gravesaner Blätter</u>, 7-8 (April 1957), 4.

167. Broder, Nathan. See Lang, Paul Henry.

168. Brooks, F.P., Jr., A.L. Hopkins, Jr., P. Newmann, and W.V. Wright. "An experiment in musical composition." <u>Institute of Radio Engineers Transactions on Electronic Computers</u>, EC-6, 3 (Sept. 1957), 175. <u>Annales des Télécommunications</u>, 100522 (Jan. 1958).

169. ------ <u>et al</u>. "Correction to 'An experiment in musical composition.'" <u>IRE Transactions on Electronic Computers</u>, EC-7, 1 (March 1958), 60.

170. Brown, B. "Why 'thinking machines' cannot think."
The New York Times, CX (Feb. 19, 1961), magazine
section, 19.

171. Brown, D. "How to make electronic music." Popular
Science, CLXXVI (April 1960), 184.

172. "Brussels: Belgian National Radio week of experimental music." World of Music, 5 (Oct. 1958), 4.

173. Bruyn, J.W. de. See Badings, Henk.

174. Bürck, W. "Betrachtungen zur stereophonen und pseu-
dostereophonen 2-Kanalwiedergabe in der Praxis"/
"Some thoughts on two-channel stereophonic and
pseudo-stereophonic reproduction in practice."
Gravesaner Blätter/Gravesano Review, IV, 15-16
(1960), 134/142.

175. Burjanek, J. "Ma nas skladatel experimentovat?"
Slovenská Hudba, V (Nov. 1961), 469.

176. Bürke, Fred. See Heck, Ludwig.

177. Burrows, David. "Current chronicle: United States
(New Haven)." The Musical Quarterly, LII, 3 (July
1966), 368.

178. Burt, F. "An anthithesis: the aesthetic aspect."
Score, 19 (March 1957), 64.

179. Busoni, Ferruccio Benvenuto. Entwurf einer neuen
Aesthetik der Tonkunst. Trieste, 1907; Leipzig,
Insel Verlag, 1910. Translated by Theodore Baker
as Sketch of a new aesthetic of music. New York,
G. Schirmer, 1911.

180. "By the numbers." Musical America, LXXVI, 11 (Sept.
1956), 13.

181. Caciotti, M., P. Righini, and Vittorio Savelli. "Un
instrument électronique pour l'accord des grands
orchestres." Annales des Télécommunications, XII
(Oct. 1957), 367.

182. Cadieu, Martine. "Duo avec Stockhausen." Nouvelles

littéraires, (June 15, 1961), 9.

183. Cage, John. "A few ideas about music and films."
     Film Music Notes, X, 3 (Jan.-Feb. 1951), 12. Film
     Culture, 29 (Summer 1963), 35.

184. ------ "For more new sounds." Modern Music, XIX, 4
     (May-June 1942), 243.

185. ------ "Four musicians at work" (Feldman, Boulez,
     Cage, Wolff). trans/formation, I, 3 (1952), 168.

186. ------ "Goal: new music, new dance." Dance Observer,
     VI (Dec. 1939), 296.

187. ------ "Grace and clarity." Dance Observer, XI (Nov.
     1944), 108.

188. ------ John Cage (catalog of works). New York,
     Henmar Press, 1962 (in collaboration with Robert
     Dunn).

189. ------ Silence. Middletown, Conn., Wesleyan Univer-
     sity Press, 1961.

190. ------ "Zur Geschichte der experimentellen Musik in
     den Vereinigten Staaten." Darmstädter Beiträge
     zur neuen Musik, II (1959). Translation by Heinz-
     Klaus Metzger of "History of experimental music in
     the United States," in Silence, 67.

191. ------ et al. "The 25-year retrospective concert
     of the music of John Cage" (notes to recordings).
     New York, George Avakian, 1959.

192. Canby, Edward T. "The composing machine." Audio
     Engineering, XXXVIII (Nov. 1954), 48.

193. ------ "Déserts, by Varèse." Audio, XXXIX (July
     1955), 28.

194. ------ "Electronics -- a side view." Audio, XLV
     (May 1961), 10.

195. ------ "Music synthesizer." Audio, XL (May 1956),
     64.

196. ------ "Pretty Cagey." Audio, XLV (Oct. 1961), 12.

197. Candra, Z. "O hudbe v cinohre, hudební moderne a avant-garde, s jubilantem Miroslavem Poncem." Hudební Rozhledy, XV, 21 (1962), 894.

198. Cardew, Cornelius. "Cologne: Nono and Earle Brown." The Musical Times, CIV (March 1963), 196.

199. Carpenter, Allan. "Amazing new uses for robot brains." Science Digest, XLI, 2 (Feb. 1957), 1.

200. Carter, Elliott and Vladimir A. Ussachevsky. "Reel vs. real." American Symphony Orchestra League Newsletter, XII (1960), 8.

201. Cary, Tristram. "Sproggletaggle." Composer, 18 (Jan. 1966), 6.

202. Castelnuovo, Gino. "Lo studio di fonologia di Radio Milano." Elettronica, V, 3 (Sept. 1956), 106.

203. Chamass, Mireille. "Analyse." Situation de la recherche, Cahiers d'études de radio-télévision, 27-28 (Sept.-Oct. 1960), 248. Paris, Flammarion.

204. Chambure, Alain de. "Infrastructure technique." La Revue musicale, 244 (1959), 51.

205. Chamfray, Claude. "Paul Arma, nous parle de son 'Concerto pour Bande Magnetique.'" Guide du concert, 293-294 (Dec. 16, 1960), 455.

206. Champernowne, D.G. "Music from EDSAC." Cambridge, England, University of Cambridge, Technical Report, 1961.

207. Chapman, E. "Electronic music." Musical Events, XVI (Dec. 1961), 28.

208. Charles, Daniel. "Entr'acte: 'formal' or 'informal' music?" In Lang and Broder, eds., Contemporary music in Europe. New York, G. Schirmer, 1965, 144. The Musical Quarterly, LI, 1 (Jan. 1965), 144.

209. Chávez, Carlos. <u>Toward a new music</u>. New York, W.W.
     Norton, 1937.

210. Cherry, E.C. <u>On human communication</u>. New York,
     John Wiley and Sons, 1957.

211. ------ ed. <u>Information theory -- third London Sym-
     posium</u>. New York, Academic Press, 1956.

212. Childs, Barney. "The newest minstrelsy: a dialogue."
     <u>Selmer Bandwagon</u>, XIII, 5 (Nov. 1965), 4.

213. ------ "What concerns me is music" (interview with
     Charles Wuorinen). <u>Genesis West</u>, 1 (Fall 1962),
     11.

214. Chou, Wen-Chung. "Varèse: a sketch of the man and
     his music." <u>The Musical Quarterly</u>, LII, 2 (April
     1966), 151.

215. Clark, Melville, Jr. "Proposed key-board musical
     instrument." <u>Journal of the Acoustical Society
     of America</u>, XXXI, 4 (1959), 403.

216. ------ "Ein neues Musikinstrument"/"A new musical
     instrument." <u>Gravesaner Blätter/Gravesano Review</u>,
     IV, 14 (1959), 92/110.

217. Clark, Robert K. "A program for the real-time
     generation of musical sounds." <u>Journal of the
     Audio Engineering Society</u>, XIV, 1 (1966), 21.

218. Claro, S. "Panorama de la música experimental en
     Chile." <u>Revista Musical Chilena</u>, XVII, 83 (1963),
     111.

219. Coeuroy, André. "Le 'Nouveau Festival 1953.'"
     <u>Cahiers d'information musicale du CDMI</u>, 9-10
     (Summer-Autumn 1953), 5.

220. Cohen, Joel E. "Information theory and music."
     <u>Behavioral Science</u>, VII, 2 (April 1962), 137.

221. Cohen, Milton J. "Space theatre." <u>Arts and Archi-
     tecture</u>, LXXIX, 8 (August 1962), 10.

222. Cohn, Arthur. "Avant-garde at the Philharmonic."
     Listen, I (March-April 1964), 20.

223. ------ "Electronic music." American Record Guide,
     XXX (June 1964), 924.

224. ------ "How to get a joint raided, and other elec-
     tronic music" (review of recording). American
     Record Guide, XXXII (August 1966), 1114.

225. ------ "The nation's music: New York." Musical
     Courier, CLXIII (June 1961), 18.

226. ------ "The new music from Germany" (review of re-
     cordings). American Record Guide, XXVI (Nov.
     1959), 176.

227. ------ "Stockhausen's Kontakte on DGG -- a telling
     experience." American Record Guide, XXIX, 12
     (August 1963), 952.

228. ------ Twentieth century music in western Europe.
     Philadelphia, Lippincott, 1965.

229. Colacicchi, Luigi. "Il Premio Italia." Musica
     d'Oggi, III, 10 (Dec. 1960), 475.

230. Collaer, Paul. La musique moderne, 1905-1955.
     Paris, Elsevier, 1955. Translated by Sally Abeles
     as A history of modern music. Cleveland, World,
     1961.

231. ------ "L'oeuvre récente des grands maîtres
     d'aujourd'hui." Cahier musicale, 2 (March 1957).

232. "Cologne: I.S.C.M." The Music Review, XXI, 3 (August
     1960), 242.

233. "Cologne: musicologists' congress: 22nd-24th October."
     The Music Review, XVI (1955), 66.

234. "Columbia-Princeton gets Rockefeller grant." Musical
     America, LXXIX (May 1959), 30.

235. "Composer -- the brain." Melody Maker, XXXI, (July
     21, 1956), 2.

236. "Composer's workshop." <u>Selmer Bandwagon</u>, XIII, 5 (Nov. 1965), 8.

237. "Composition for tape recorder (Dartington Summer School of Music)." <u>Musical Events</u>, XVI (Nov. 1961), 16.

238. "Computer makes music of trumpet sounds." <u>Science News Letter</u>, LXXXVIII (Dec. 11, 1965), 375.

239. "Computer produces trumpet sounds." <u>Journal of the Acoustical Society of America</u>, XXXIX, 4 (April 1966), 760.

240. "Concert de musique expérimentale." <u>The Musical Times</u>, C (Jan. 1959), 30.

241. Conly, John M. "The composer's new tool." <u>High Fidelity</u>, VII, 2 (Feb. 1957), 33.

242. "Contactorgaan electronische muziek C.E.M." <u>Sonorum Speculum</u>, 16 (Sept. 1963).

243. "Contemporary music by Cage and Varèse." <u>Musical America</u>, LXXVIII, 5 (May 1959), 30.

244. Cony, Ed. "Canny computers -- machines write music, play checkers, tackle new tasks in industry." <u>Wall Street Journal</u>, CXLVIII, 56 (Sept. 19, 1956), 1.

245. Copley, I.A. "On the dictatorship of the minority; some uncharitable reflections." <u>Making Music</u>, 52 (Summer 1963), 10.

246. "Copyrighting soundtrack score." <u>Variety</u>, CCXI (August 27, 1958), 43.

247. Le Corbusier (pseudonym). See Jeanneret-Gris, Charles-Édouard.

248. Cordonnier, J.G. "Stereophonische Klangweidergabe." <u>Gravesaner Blätter</u>, 6-7 (April 1957), 9.

249. "Court historique de la recherche a la Radiodiffusion-télévision francaise." <u>Situation de la recherche</u>,

Cahiers d'études de radio-télévision, 27-28 (Sept.-
Dec. 1960), 5. Paris, Flammarion.

250. Cowell, Henry. "Composing with tape." Hi-Fi Music
at Home, II (Jan.-Feb. 1956), 23.

251. ------ "Current chronicle: New York." The Musical
Quarterly, XXXVIII, 4 (Oct. 1952), 597.

252. ------ "Current chronicle: New York." The Musical
Quarterly, XXXIX, 2 (April 1953), 254.

253. Craft, Robert. See Stravinsky, Igor.

254. "Criticism by machine." Time, LXVIII (July 30,
1956), 56.

255. Cross, D. "Music vs. electronics." Hi-Fi Music at
Home, VI (April 1959), 19.

256. Crosson, F.J. See Sayre, K.M.

257. Crowhurst, Norman H. Electronic musical instrument
handbook. Indianapolis, Howard W. Sams, 1962.

258. ------ Electronic musical instrument handbook.
Reviewed in Clavier, I, 4 (1962), 6.

259. ------ Electronic musical instrument handbook.
Reviewed in The Instrumentalist, XVII, 2 (Oct.
1962), 8.

260. ------ Electronic musical instrument handbook. Reviewed in Music Educators Journal, XLIX, 2 (Nov.-
Dec. 1962), 122.

261. Cunningham, E. "Music and the Olympics: Tokyo 1964."
Musical America, LXXXIV (Dec. 1964), 36.

262. Curjel, Hans. "Wandlungen des tönenden Materials."
Melos, XXXI, 11 (Nov. 1964), 342.

263. "La cybernétique et la musique." Musica Disques,
CI (August 1962), 58.

264. Czerny, P. "Technische Revolution und Musik."

Musik und Gesellschaft, XIV (April 1964), 193.

265. Dahlhaus, Carl and Rudolf Stephan. "Eine dritte
Epoche der Musik." *Deutsche Universitäts-Zeitung*,
X (Sept. 12, 1955), 14.

266. Dallapiccola, Luigi. "Besuch in Gravesano"/"Gravesano
visit." *Gravesaner Blätter/Gravesano Review*, III,
10 (1958), 2.

267. Daniel, N.I. "Electronic music." *Communications*,
XX, 7 (July 1940), 26.

268. Daniel, O. "Anarchy and order: Dockstader's eight
electronic pieces." *Saturday Review*, XLVI (Oct.
26, 1963), 73.

269. ------ "The science of saying nothing." *Saturday
Review*, XLIX (April 30, 1966), 63.

270. Daniels, Arthur. "Report from New York: First annual conference of the American Society of University Composers." *Current Musicology*, (Spring
1966), 71.

271. "Danish radio: eight concerts." *World of Music*,
2 (July 1959), 32.

272. Danler, Karl-Robert. "Absurd -- auf die Spitze ge-
trieben." *Musica*, XVII, 2 (1963), 87.

273. ------ "Experimentelle Musik." *Musica*, 2 (1964),
76.

274. "Darmstadt report: note on musique concrète and electronic music." *Musical Courier*, CXLVIII, 5 (Oct.
15, 1953), 16.

275. Darrell, R.D. "The ersatz melody." *Saturday Review*,
XXXVIII (April 30, 1955), 64.

276. ------ "Luening and Ussachevsky: tape recorder music"
(review of recording). *High Fidelity*, VI, 9 (Sept.
1956), 95.

277. Davies, Hugh. "A discography of electronic music

and musique concrète." <u>Recorded Sound</u>, 14 (April 1964), 205. Supplement, <u>Recorded Sound</u>, 22-23 (April-July 1966), 69.

278. ------ "Letters: electronic Moscow." <u>Music and Musicians</u>, 11 (June 1963), 3.

279. ------ "<u>Die Reihe</u> reconsidered." <u>Composer</u>, 15 (Spring 1965), 20; 16 (July 1965), 17 (refutation of 58).

280. Degen, Dietz. "Das Trautonium." <u>Die Musik</u>, XXXIII (Oct. 1940-March 1941), 90.

281. "Delft: Studio voor elektronische muziek." <u>Mens en Melodie</u>, XII (Oct. 1957), 322.

282. Deliège, Celestin. "Bibliographie." <u>Revue Belge de Musicologie</u>, XIII, 1-4 (1959), 149.

283. Demarquez, Suzanne. "Paris notes." <u>Musical Courier</u>, CLVI, 3 (Feb. 1961), 27.

284. ------ "Paris première: la musique électronique" (Paul Arma). <u>Guide du concert</u>, 313 (May 12, 1961), 1093.

285. ------ "Première biennale de la recherche." <u>Guide du concert</u>, 279-280 (July 1, 1960), 891.

286. ------ "Recent trends in French music." <u>Musical Courier</u>, CLI (June 1955), 14.

287. Dennington, Arthur. "Musique concrète." <u>The Chesterian</u>, XXXI, 190 (Spring 1957), 126.

288. Deutsch, Babette. "Electronic concert." <u>Columbia University Forum</u>, III, 3 (Summer 1963), 43.

289. Deutsch, Herbert A. "A seminar in electronic music composition." <u>Journal of the Audio Engineering Society</u>, XIV, 1 (Jan. 1966), 30.

290. Deutschman, Ben. "Music from mathematics." <u>Music Journal</u>, XXII (Oct. 1964), 54.

291. Dickenson, Peter. "New York." <u>The Musical Times</u>, CII (July 1961), 440.

292. Diether, J. "Electronic music from Japan." **Musical America**, LXXXI (June 1961), 45.

293. Dietz, O. "Elektrische Musik." **Deutsche Elektrotechnik**, VII (Feb. 1953), 77.

294. Discus (pseudonym). "Music in the round: does anybody need the avant-garde?" **Harper's Magazine**, CCXXXII, 1393 (June 1966), 108.

295. Divilbiss, J.L. "The real-time generation of music with a digital computer." **Journal of Music Theory**, VIII (Spring 1964), 99.

296. Döhl, Friedhelm. "Wege der neuen Musik: zur Entwicklung der seriellen, elektronischen und experimentellen Musik." **Neue Zeitschrift für Musik**, CXXVI (March 1965), 105. **Das Orchester**, XIII (April 1965), 124.

297. "Donnell Library Center, N.Y.C.: Ussachevsky." **Bulletin of American Composers Alliance**, X (Dec. 1962), 7.

298. Dorf, Richard H. **Electronic musical instruments**. Mineola, N.Y., Radio Magazines, Inc. (Audio Library No. 1), 1954. New York, Radiofile, 1963.

299. ------ **Electronic musical instruments**. Reviewed by D.W. Martin in **Journal of the Acoustical Society of America**, XXVII (1955), 981.

300. ------ "Electronics and music." **Radio Electronics**, XXI (July 1950), 48; (August 1950), 42; XXII (Oct. 1950), 45; (Nov. 1950), 28; (Jan. 1951), 110; (May 1951), 48; (June 1951), 45; (July 1951), 44; (August 1951), 40; XXIII (March 1952), 38; (June 1952), 44; (July 1952), 48. **Annales des Télécommunications**, V, 34114 (Dec. 1950); VII, 48449 (Sept. 1952); 49044 (Oct. 1952).

301. Doschek, A. "Pittsburgh." **Musical Leader**, 96 (May 1964), 17.

302. Douglas, Alan L.M. "Compton electrone." **Electronic Engineering**, XXIII (June 1951), 226.

303. ------ "The electrical production of music." Journal
of the Audio Engineering Society, VI, 3 (July 1958),
146. Annales des Télécommunications, L 4870 (Nov.
1958).

304. ------ The electrical production of music. London,
MacDonald, 1957. New York, Philosophical Library,
1957.

305. ------ The electrical production of music. Reviewed
by Herbert Reich in Journal of Music Theory, I, 2
(Nov. 1957), 225.

306. ------ The electrical production of music. Reviewed
in The Instrumentalist, XI (June 1957), 10.

307. ------ The electrical production of music. Reviewed
in Melody Maker, XXXII (Feb. 23, 1957), 8.

308. ------ The electrical production of music. Reviewed
in Notes, XIV, 3 (June 1957), 366.

309. ------ "The electrical synthesis of music." Discovery, XXII, 2 (1961), 56. Referativnyi Zhurnal
Fizika, 11ZH652, 11 (1961).

310. ------ "The electrical synthesis of musical tones."
Electronic Engineering, XXV (July 1953), 278;
(August 1953), 336; (Sept. 1953), 370.

311. ------ "Electronic music generators." Electronic
Engineering, XXVII, 330 (August 1955), 350; 331
(Sept. 1955), 410.

312. ------ The electronic musical instrument manual.
London and New York, Pitman, 1949, 1954, 1958,
1962.

313. ------ The electronic musical instrument manual.
Reviewed by Herbert Reich in Journal of Music
Theory, I, 2 (May 1957), 225.

314. ------ The electronic musical instrument manual.
Reviewed by Raymond Suffield in The Musical Times,
XCVIII, 1371 (May 1957), 256.

315. ------ The electronic musical instrument manual.
     Reviewed in Electronics, XXIV, 6 (June 1951),
     286.

316. ------ The electronic musical instrument manual.
     Reviewed in Musical Opinion, LXXX, 958 (July 1957),
     601.

317. ------ The electronic musical instrument manual.
     Reviewed in Notes, XIV, 3 (June 1957), 366.

318. ------ "Electronic musical instruments in Germany."
     Electronic Engineering, XXX (Nov. 1958), 642.
     Annales des Télécommunications, 108359 (Oct. 1958).

319. ------ "Frequency division circuits for musical in-
     struments." Electronic Engineering, XXXII, 391
     (1960), 546.

320. ------ "Gas tubes as music generators." Electronic
     Engineering, XXXI (Nov. 1959), 672. Annales des
     Télécommunications, 123258 (Jan. 1960).

321. ------ "Improvements in electronic music generators."
     Electronic Engineering, XXXIII (Sept. 1961), 574.

322. ------ "Percussion circuits for electronic musical
     instruments." Electronic Engineering, XXX (July
     1958), 420. Annales des Télécommunications,
     108359 (Oct. 1958).

323. ------ "Recent developments in electrical music pro-
     duction." Proceedings of the Royal Musical
     Association, 83 (1956-57), 65.

324. ------ Simple electronic musical instruments for the
     constructor. London, Norman Price, 1955.

325. ------ "Solovox: novel electronic musical instrument."
     Electronic Engineering, XXII (July 1950), 275.

326. ------ "Some electronic extensions to music genera-
     ting systems." Electronic Engineering, XXXV,
     429 (Nov. 1963), 726. Annales des Télécommunica-
     tions, XII, 67243 (1963).

327. ------ "Some unusual devices for electronic music."
     Electronic Engineering, XXXI (July 1959), 419.
     Annales des Télécommunications, 120432 (Oct. 1959).

328. ------ "Synthetic music." Electronic Engineering,
     XXVIII (May 1956), 208. Annales des Télécommuni-
     cations, 84891 (July-August 1956).

329. ------ "Vibrato circuits for electrical musical in-
     struments." Electronic Engineering, XXX (Jan.
     1958), 26. Annales des Télécommunications, 102876
     (April 1958).

330. Drew, David. "Music that cannot be played: musique
     concrète." Music and Musicians, II (March 1954),
     11.

331. Driesch, Kurt. "Neues von der Elektronenmusik."
     Zeitschrift für Musik, CXV (August 1954), 473.

332. Dumm, Robert W. "Boston." The Music Magazine and
     Musical Courier, CXLIII (Nov. 1961), 60.

333. Dunn, Robert. See Cage, John.

334. Eggeling, Helmut. "Die neue Instrumente." Melos,
     XX (Jan. 1953), 13.

335. Ehle, Robert C. "An integrated complex-tone gene-
     rator for electronic music." Audio, L, 10 (Oct.
     1966), 81.

336. Ehringer, H. "Klangzauberer treffen sich in Basel."
     Melos, XXII (July-August 1955), 230.

337. Eibner, Franz. "Die Verwendung elektro-akustischer
     Instrumente beim Gottdeinst." Bericht, Interna-
     tional Kongress für Katholisches Kirchenmusik,
     1955, 320.

338. Eimert, Herbert. "Electronic music." Ottawa,
     National Research Council of Canada, Technical
     Translation TT-601, 1956 (translation of 341).

339. ------ "Elektronische Musik." In Die Musik in
     Geschichte und Gegenwart, III. Kassel, Bärenreiter,

1954, 1263.

340. ------ "Die elektronische Musik." Oesterreichische
Musikzeitschrift, XVI (June-July 1961), 316.

341. ------ "Elektronische Musik." Technische Hausmitteilungen des Nordwestdeutschen Rundfunks, VI,
1-2 (1954), 4.

342. ------ "Estetica della musica elettronica." La
Rassegna musicale, XXXI, 4 (1961), 325.

343. ------ "Fragenwürdiges in einer Geschichte der modernen Musik." Melos, XXXI (June 1964), 190.

344. ------ "Die Franzosen sprechen nicht mehr von Musique
concrète." Melos, XXXIII, 9 (Sept. 1966), 280.

345. ------ "Der Komponist und die elektronischen Klangmittel." Das Musikleben, VII (July-August 1954),
242.

346. ------ "Möglichkeiten und Grenzen der elektronischen
Musik." Schweizerische Musikzeitung, XCIII (Nov.
1953), 445.

347. ------ "Musique électronique." La Revue musicale,
236 (1957), 45.

348. ------ "Nachruf auf Werner Meyer-Eppler." Die Reihe,
VIII (1962), 5.

349. ------ "The place of electronic music in the musical
situation." Ottawa, National Research Council of
Canada, Technical Translation TT-610, 1956 (translation of 355).

350. ------ "Die sieben Stücke"/"What is electronic music?" Die Reihe, I/1 (1955/1958), 8/1.

351. ------ "Der Sinus-Ton." Melos, XXI (June 1954), 168.

352. ------ "Was ist elektronische Musik?" Melos, XX,
1 (Jan. 1953), 1.

353. ------ "Von der Entscheidungsfreiheit des Komponis-

ten"/"The composer's freedom of choice." <u>Die Reihe</u>, III/3 (1957/1959), 5/1.

354. ------ "Zur Aesthetik der elektronischen Musik." <u>Revue Belge de Musicologie</u>, XIII, 1-4 (1959), 50.

355. ------ "Zur musikalischen Situation." <u>Technische Hausmitteilungen des Nordwestdeutschen Rundfunks</u>, VI, 1-2 (1954), 42.

356. ------ Fritz Enkel, and Karlheinz Stockhausen. "Fragen der Notation elektronischen Musik." <u>Technische Hausmitteilungen des Nordwestdeutschen Rundfunks</u>, VI, 1-2 (1954), 52.

357. ------, ------, and ------ "Problems of electronic music notation." Ottawa, National Research Council of Canada, Technical Translation TT-612, 1956 (translation of 356).

358. "Electronic age opens many vistas in music." <u>Musical Courier</u>, CXLV (Jan. 1, 1952), 6.

359. "An electronic ballet (Gassman's 'Electronics')." <u>American Record Guide</u>, XXVIII (Feb. 1962), 464.

360. "Electronic brain composes at University of Illinois." <u>Illinois Music Educator</u>, XVI, 1 (Sept.-Oct. 1956), 16.

361. "Electronic lost chord?" <u>Musical America</u>, LXXX (June 1960), 13.

362. "Electronic medley." <u>Time</u>, LXV, 23 (June 6, 1955), 78.

363. "Electronic music." In <u>The International Cyclopedia of Music and Musicians</u>, 9th ed. New York, Dodd, Mead and Co., 1964, 594.

364. "Electronic music -- a bibliography." New York, Columbia-Princeton Electronic Music Center, revised, December 4, 1961 (mimeograph).

365. "Electronic-music courses offered at the University of Toronto." <u>Journal of the Acoustical Society</u>

of America, XXXIX, 4 (April 1966), 772.

366. "Electronic music grant." National Music Council Bulletin, XX, 2 (1960), 33.

367. "Electronic music: news and comments." Score, 11 (March 1955), 67.

368. "Electronic music: news and comments." Score, 15 (March 1956), 83.

369. "The electronic music studio in Brussels." Brussels, Ministry of Foreign Affairs and External Trade (Memo from Belgium No. 39), Nov. 15, 1965.

370. "Electronic music subject of grant." The New York Times, CVIII (Jan. 18, 1959), section 1, 9.

371. Electronic musical instruments, a bibliography, 2nd ed. London, Tottenham Public Libraries and Museum, 1952.

372. Electronic musical instruments, a bibliography. Reviewed in Journal of the Acoustical Society of America, XXIV (1952), 420.

373. "Electronic pencil enables composers to hear score." Journal of the Acoustical Society of America, XXI (Jan. 1949), 63. Summary in Science News Letter, LIV (Nov. 13, 1948), 309.

374. "Electronic virtuoso: RCA electronic music synthesizer." Newsweek, XLV (Feb. 7, 1955), 70.

375. "Electronophone?" Musical America, LXXIV (Feb. 1, 1954), 6.

376. "Elektricheskie muzykal'nye instrumenty." Sovetskaya Muzyka, XXV (Feb. 1961), 203.

377. "Elektrische Musik." Funk Technik, 2 (1949), 661. Annales des Télécommunications, V, 29408 (April 1950).

378. "Elektrogene Musik." Musica Schallplatte, 1 (1958), 9.

379. "Elektronenmesse von Hermann Heiss." <u>Singende Kirche</u>,
XII, 3 (1965), 133.

380. "Elektronische Musik." <u>Melos</u>, XXV (June 1958), 211.

381. "Elektronische Musik. Eine Zeitgemässe Tagung in
Trossingen." <u>Instrumentenbau Zeitschrift</u>, VII
(1953), 85.

382. "Elektronische Musik in Italien." <u>Melos</u>, XXIV (May
1957), 139.

383. "Elektronische Musikgeräte." <u>Elektrotechnische
Zeitschrift</u>, VI B (August 21, 1954), 305.

384. "Elektronische Muziek." <u>Mens en Melodie</u>, XII (Dec.
1957), 395.

385. "Elektronisierte Schlager." <u>Melos</u>, XXVI (Feb. 1959),
57.

386. "Endlich kann in München die Avantgarde experimen-
tieren." <u>Melos</u>, XXX (March 1963), 94.

387. Enkel, Fritz. "Elektroakustische Mittel zur Darstellung von Hörspielgeräuschen." <u>Technische Hausmitteilungen des Nordwestdeutschen Rundfunks</u>, V (March-
April 1953), 47. <u>Annales des Télécommunications</u>,
VIII, 57658 (Oct. 1953).

388. ------ "Das neue Klangmaterial." <u>Gravesaner Blätter</u>,
6 (Dec. 1956), 20.

389. ------ "The technical facilities of the electronic
music studio (of the Cologne Broadcasting Station)."
Ottawa, National Research Council of Canada, Technical Translation TT-603, 1956 (translation of
391).

390. ------ "Die Technik des Tonstudios." In Winckel,
ed., <u>Klangstruktur der Musik</u>. Berlin, Verlag für
Radio-Foto-Kinotechnik, 1955, 159.

391. ------ "Die technischen Einrichtungen des 'Studios
für elektronische Musik.'" <u>Technische Hausmitteilungen des Nordwestdeutschen Rundfunks</u>, VI, 1-2

(1954), 8.

392. ------ See Eimert, Herbert.

393. ------ and Heinz Schütz. "Die Herstellung von Hörspielgeräuschen." <u>Technische Hausmitteilungen des
Nordwestdeutschen Rundfunks</u>, VI, 1-2 (1954), 40.

394. ------ and ------ "Magnetic-tape technique (of recording electronic music)." Ottawa, National Research Council of Canada, Technical Translation
TT-604, 1956 (translation 396).

395. ------ and ------ "The production of sound effects
for radio dramas." Ottawa, National Research
Council of Canada, Technical Translation TT-609,
1956 (translation of 393).

396. ------ and ------ "Zur Technik des Magnettonbandes."
<u>Technische Hausmitteilungen des Nordwestdeutschen
Rundfunks</u>, VI, 1-2 (1954), 16.

397. "Entretiens et débats à l'occasion du Nouveau Festival 1953." <u>Cahiers d'information musicale du
CDMI</u>, 9-10 (Summer-Autumn 1953), 11.

398. Erismann, G. "Magie et verité des sons (entretien
avec Michel Philippot)." <u>Musica</u> (Chaix), 130
(Jan. 1965), 26.

399. "Ersatz earfuls." <u>Newsweek</u>, LIII (Jan. 26, 1959),
91.

400. Essex, J.W. "Electronic music is here." <u>Radio-
Electronics</u>, XXXIV, 2 (1963), 49.

401. Evangelisti, Franco. "Verso una composizione elettronica." <u>Ordini</u>, 1 (July 1959).

402. Evarts, John. "Electronic experimentation flourish-
ing." <u>World of Music</u>, 3 (Oct. 1959), 45.

403. Ewen, David. <u>David Ewen introduces modern music</u>.
Philadelphia and New York, Chilton, 1962, 277.

404. "Experiment oder manier?" <u>Hausmusik</u>, XVI, (July-

Oct. 1952), 141.

405. "Experimental studio at Gravesano of Hermann Scherchen." World of Music, III, 3 (June 1961).

406. Eyer, Ronald. "Works for tape recorder played in Stokowski concerts." Musical America, LXXII (Nov. 15, 1952), 8.

407. Fahlstrom, Oyvind. "Ljuv hetsig dalighet i konstens tjanst." Expressen (Stockholm), (Nov. 13, 1960), 4.

408. Faltin, P. "Clovek-technika-umenie (pokus o uvahu filozofujucu)." Slovenská Hudba, VIII, 4 (1964), 100.

409. "Far-out at the Philharmonic: bangs and gurgles." Time, LXXXIII (Feb. 14, 1964), 79.

410. Fastenaekels, V. "Electronic music." Radio-Electronics, XXIII (Dec. 1952), 39.

411. "Father: music without instruments or electronic music." The New Yorker, XXXIX (Jan. 18, 1964), 25.

412. Ferentzy, E.N. and M. Havass. "Human movement analysis by computer -- electronic choreography and music composition." In Computational Linguistics, III. Budapest, Computing Centre of the Hungarian Academy of Sciences, 1964.

413. Ferrari, Luc. "Les étapes de la production." La Revue musicale, 244 (1959), 54.

414. ------ "Les manipulations." Situation de la recherche, Cahiers d'études de radio-télévision, 27-28 (Sept.-Oct. 1960), 244. Paris, Flammarion.

415. ------ "Tautologos I." Gravesaner Blätter/Gravesano Review, 27-28 (Nov. 1965), 105/106.

416. Ferretti, Ercolino. "Exploration and organization of sound with the computer" (abstract). Journal of the Acoustical Society of America, XXXIX, 6 (June 1966), 1245.

417. Feschotte, Jacques. "Musique concrète, peinture abstraite, art brut." Feuilles musicaux, 9 (Nov. 1955).

418. Fierz, G. "Studio-reihe neuer Musik" (review of recordings). Schweizerische Musikzeitung, CIV, 3 (1964), 190.

419. "The first ballad to be composed by an electronic computer." International Musician, LV (Aug. 1956), 21.

420. Fleming, E.D. "Recognize talent if you see it." Cosmopolitan, CXLIX (Sept. 1960), 54.

421. Fleuret, Maurice. "Pierre Henry." Guide du concert, 393 (June 22, 1963), 14.

422. Florian, L. "Experimentalne hudobne nastroje a moderna technika." Slovenská Hudba, VI (Feb. 1962), 41.

423. Fokker, Adriaan Daniel. "Wozu und warum?" Die Reihe, VIII (1962), 62.

424. ------ Recherches musicales, théoriques et pratiques. The Hague, 1951.

425. Forte, Allen. "Composing with electrons in Cologne." High Fidelity, VI (Oct. 1956), 64.

426. Foss, Lucas. "The changing composer-performer relationship: a monologue and a dialogue." Perspectives of New Music, I, 2 (Spring 1963), 45.

427. Fränkel, S. "Internationales Kolloquium über elektronische Musik in Gent." Schweizerische Musikzeitung, CIV, 6 (1964), 374.

428. Frankenstein, Alfred. "The 'big and spacious music' of Edgard Varèse" (record review of Poème électronique). High Fidelity, X, 10 (Oct. 1960), 69.

429. ------ "Luening, Otto; Ussachevsky, Vladimir: tape recorder music" (review of recording). High Fidelity, V, 4 (June 1955), 58.

33

430. —————— "Stimulating sounds from the concrete mixers of Paris." <u>High Fidelity</u>, VII (Feb. 1957), 82.

431. —————— "Vortex: the music of the hemispheres." <u>High Fidelity</u>, IX, 5 (May 1959), 45.

432. Freitas Branco, Joao de. "A 'musica concreta': proposito dos espectaculos de Maurice Béjart." <u>Arte Musical</u>, XXVII (August 1959), 136.

433. —————— "Novos concietos musicais e suas relacionacoes com a Ciencia." <u>Arte Musical</u>, XXIX, 18 (1962), 41.

434. French, R.F. "Current chronicle: New York." <u>The Musical Quarterly</u>, L, 3 (1964), 382.

435. Freyse, R. "Panorama der neuen Musik." <u>Neue Zeitschrift für Musik</u>, CXXV, 7-8 (1964), 356.

436. Frisch, B.H. "This man is composing music: electronic music." <u>Science Digest</u>, LVII (Feb. 1965), 72.

437. "Fritz Enkel" (obituary). <u>Gravesaner Blätter/Gravesano Review</u>, IV, 15-16 (1960), 4.

438. "From Minerva House." <u>Musical Opinion</u>, LXXXI (May 1958), 501.

439. Fucks, Wilhelm. "Gibt es mathematische Gesetze in Sprache und Musik." <u>Umschau</u>, LVII, 2 (1957), 33.

440. —————— "Mathematische Analyse der Formalstruktur von Musik." In <u>Forschungsbericht des Ministeriums für Wirtschaft und Verkehr des Landes NWR</u>, No. 357. Köln und Opladen, Westdeutscher Verlag, 1958. "Mathematical analysis of formal structure of music," <u>Institute of Radio Engineers Transactions on Information Theory</u>, IT-8, 5 (Sept. 1962), 225.

441. —————— "Mathematische Analyse von Formalstrukturen von Werken der Musik." <u>Arbeitsgemeinschaft für Forschung des Landes NRW</u>, No. 124. Köln und Opladen, Westdeutscher Verlag, 1963.

442. ------ "Mathematische Analyse von Werken der Sprache und der Musik." <u>Physikalische Blätter</u>, XVI, 9 (1960), 452.

443. ------ "Mathematische Musikanalyse und Randomfolgen. Musik und Zufall"/"Musical analysis by mathematics. Random sequences. Music by accident." <u>Gravesaner Blätter/Gravesano Review</u>, VI, 23-24 (1962), 132/146.

444. ------ "Über mathematische Musikanalyse." <u>Nachrichtentechnische Zeitschrift</u>, XVII, 2 (1964), 41.

445. Fujita, Hisashi. See Takatsuji, Tsukasa.

446. Füssl, K.H. "Elektronische 'Première' in Wien." <u>Oesterreichische Musikzeitschrift</u>, XIII (Jan. 1958), 34.

447. Gabura, A.J. "Computer analysis of musical style." <u>ACM Proceedings, 20th National Conference</u>. New York, Association for Computing Machinery, 1965, 303.

448. Galpin, Francis W. "The music of electricity." <u>Proceedings of the Royal Musical Association</u>, LXIV (1938), 71.

449. Gelatt, Roland. "Music makers" (RCA Synthesizer). <u>High Fidelity</u>, V (August 1955), 41.

450. "The generating and distributing of music by means of alternators." <u>Electrical World</u>, XLVII, 10 (March 10, 1906), 519.

451. Gentil, K. "Das 'Flex a Tone' und die 'Singende Säge.'" <u>Acustica</u>, VII, 1 (1957), 58.

452. Genzmer, Harald. "Das Mixtur-Trautonium." <u>Das Musikleben</u>, VII (1954), 245.

453. Gerbes, H. "Neue Musik und neuzeitliches Denken." <u>Schweizerische Musikzeitung</u>, CIV, 4 (1964), 231.

454. Gerhard, Roberto. "Concrète and electronic sound composition." In <u>Music libraries and instruments</u>.

London, Hinrichsen Edition, 1961 (Hinrichsen's Eleventh Music Book), 31.

455. Gernsback, Hugo. "Micromusic: electronics is the mother of future music." Radio-Electronics, XXX (March 1959), 35.

456. Gill, S. "A technique for the composition of music in a computer." Computer Journal, VI, 2 (July 1963), 129.

457. Gilmore, Ken. "Dig that crazy music." Electronics Illustrated, (Nov. 1962), 84.

458. Giovaninetti, Reynald. "Musiques expérimentales." Situation de la recherche, Cahiers d'études de radio-télévision, 27-28 (Sept.-Dec. 1960), 57. Paris, Flammarion.

459. Givelet, A. "Les instruments de musique à oscillations électriques," Genie Civil, (Sept. 22, 1928).

460. Glanville-Hicks, Peggy. "Tapesichord: the music of whistle and bang." Vogue, CXXII (July 1953), 80.

461. Goeyvaerts, Karel. "Das elektronische Klangmaterial", "The sound material of electronic music." Die Reihe, I/1 (1955/1958), 14/35.

462. Goldberg, Albert. "New sounds and new works in Los Angeles." Musical America, LXXV (Jan. 1955), 42.

463. Goldman, Richard Franko. "Current chronicle: New York." The Musical Quarterly, XLVII, 3 (1961), 396.

464. ------ "Current chronicle: New York." The Musical Quarterly, XLVIII, 1 (1962), 93.

465. ------ "Percy Grainger's 'free music' (Cross-Grainger instrument)." Juilliard Review, II (Fall 1955), 42.

466. Goldsmith, Alfred N. "Chávez on music and electricity." Modern Music, XIV (1937), 164.

467. ------ "Electricity becomes music." Modern Music,
     XV, 1 (1937), 17.

468. Goléa, Antoine. "Deux portraits." In La musique
     et ses problèmes contemporains 1953-1963. Paris,
     René Julliard (Cahiers de la Compagnie Madelaine
     Renaud -- Jean-Louis Barrault, 41), 1963, 124.

469. ------ "French music since 1945." In Lang and
     Broder, eds., Contemporary music in Europe, New
     York, G. Schirmer, 1965, 22. The Musical Quarterly,
     LI, 1 (Jan. 1965), 22.

470. ------ "Grenzgebiete der Musik." Neue Zeitschrift
     für Musik, CXXII (Oct. 1961), 421.

471. ------ "Im Drahtverhau des drei Klangsystems."
     Melos, XXIII (1956), 164.

472. ------ "Tendances de la musique concrète." La Revue
     musicale, 236 (1957), 36.

473. ------ Vingt ans de musique contemporaine. Paris,
     Seghers, 1962.

474. Goodell, J.D. "Electronic composition of music."
     Radio News, Radio-Electronic Dept., V (July 1945),
     12, 44.

475. Goslich, Herbert. "Das Klangreich." Das Musikleben,
     VI (1953), 213.

476. Götz, Karl Otto. "Vom abstrakten Film zur Elektro-
     nenmalerei." In Movens. Wiesbaden, Limes Verlag,
     1960.

477. Gould, Glenn. "The prospects of recording." High
     Fidelity, XVI, 4 (April 1966), 46.

478. Gradenwitz, Peter. "Experiments in sound." New
     York Times, CII, 5 (August 9, 1953), section 2.

479. ------ "Experiments in sound: ten-day demonstration
     in Paris offers the latest in 'musique concrète.'"
     Bulletin of American Composers Alliance, III, 3
     (1953), 12.

480. ------ "Israel: Exodus by Josef Tal, performace by
     the Broadcasting Service." Musical Courier, CLVII
     (May 1958), 37.

481. "Graphs: electrically generated frequencies in terms
     of intensity and time." Music and Musicians, VII,
     1 (Sept. 1958), 9.

482. Gräter, M. Konzertführer: neue Musik. Frankfurt
     and Hamburg, Fischer Bücherei, 1955.

483. "Gravesano, workshop sponsored by the Swiss radio."
     World of Music, III, 6 (Dec. 1961), 144.

484. Graziotin, I. "Premesse di eufonotechnica teorica
     per la construzione di un compositore automatico
     di musica combinatore di polifoni e di uno stru-
     mento totale." Antenna, XXVII (July 1953), 182,
     196. Annales des Télécommunications, 78385 (Nov.
     1955).

485. Gredinger, Paul. "Das Serielle"/"Serial technique."
     Die Reihe, I/1 (1955/1958), 34/38.

486. Green, Bert F., Jr. "Non-computational uses of di-
     gital computers." Behavioral Science, IV, 2
     (April 1959), 164.

487. Greenlee, L.E. "Electron music with Fototone."
     Radio Craft, XIX (August 1948), 30.

488. Gregory, Robin. "Music by machine." Musical Opi-
     nion, LXXXII, 973 (Oct. 1958), 21.

489. Gross, C. "'There's been nothing since the classics'
     (?); of odd birds, Cage, and 'chance music.'"
     Listen, I (March-April 1964), 1.

490. "Le groupe de recherches de musique concrète."
     La Revue musicale, 236 (1957), 135.

491. Grunfeld, Frederic. "Adventures in sound: the well-
     tempered ionizer." High Fidelity, IV, 7 (Sept.
     1954), 39.

492. ------ "The wizard of Gravesano." HiFi/Stereo

Review, VII (Sept. 1961), 35.

493. "Gulbransen piano used as electronic brain writes
1,000 popular songs an hour." Piano Revue, CXV
(Sept 1956), 21.

494. Günther, Siegfried. "Die Gesellschaft als Ursache
und Wirkfeld der Neuen Musik." Schweizerische
Musikzeitung, CIII, 1 (1963), 2.

495. ------ "Grenzziehungen." Musica, XVII, 4 (1963),
181.

496. ------ "Der Menschheit Würde ist in eure Hand ge-
geben ... " Das Orchester, X (April 1962), 116.

497. Guttman, N. "Über die Computer-Musik-Beispiele"/
"Notes on computer music examples." Gravesaner
Blätter/Gravesano Review, VI, 23-24 (1962), 126/
129.

498. ------ See Mathews, Max V.

499. Guy, Percival J. "Musique concrète and radiophonics." In Practical Tape Recording. London,
Norman Price, 1964, 39.

500. Guyonnet, Jacques. "Structures et communication."
In La musique et ses problèmes contemporains
1953-1963. Paris, René Julliard (Cahiers de la
Compagnie Madeleine Renaud -- Jean-Louis Barrault,
41), 1963, 270.

501. Haase, Kurt H. See Meyer-Eppler, Werner, ed.

502. Hadden, George H. "Some considerations regarding
volume production of electronic musical instruments." Journal of the Audio Engineering Society,
I (Jan. 1953), 29.

503. Halffter, Cristóbal. "La música concreta." Pro
Arte Musical, VII (Oct. 1955), 67.

504. Halford, F. "Music in Germany." Canon, XV (June
1962), 9.

505. Hamel, Fred. See Thienhaus, Erich.

506. Hansell, S.H. "Elektronische Experimente östlich
     des Mississippi." Melos, 29, XXIX (Dec. 1962),
     388.

507. Hansen, Peter S. An introduction to twentieth cen-
     tury music. Boston, Allyn and Bacon, 1961, 345.

508. Hansen, William D. "This is music." Chicago Tri-
     bune, CXVIII, 15 (April 12, 1959), magazine sec-
     tion, 43.

509. Hanson, Howard. "Musical needs and the search for
     new resources" (abstract). Journal of the Acous-
     tical Society of America, XXIX (1957), 770.

510. Harrison, J.S. "The New York music scene." Musical
     America, LXXXIV (March 1964), 24.

511. Hartmann, Karl. Versuch einer mathematischen Musik-
     lehre. Wien, Hartmann, 1962.

512. Hassan, Ihab. "The dismemberment of Orpheus." The
     American Scholar, XXXII (1963), 463.

513. Havass, M. "A simulation of musical composition."
     In Computational Linguistics, III. Budapest,
     Computing Centre of the Hungarian Academy of
     Sciences, 1964, 107.

514. ------- See Ferentzy, E.N.

515. Hayoz, J.M. "En quête d'objectivité." Schweizer-
     ische Musikzeitung, CI, 2 (1961), 97.

516. Hearne, H. "Electronic production of percussive
     sounds." Journal of the Audio Engineering Soci-
     ety, IX (Oct. 1961), 270.

517. Heck, Ludwig. "Die erste elektronische Partitur"
     (Studie II by Karlheinz Stockhausen). Melos,
     XXIII (Nov. 1956), 316.

518. ------- "Klangsynthese durch elektronische Bildabtas-
     tung." Elektrotechnische Zeitschrift, B XIII, 17

(1961), 454.

519. ------ and Fred Bürck. "Klänge im Schmeltztiegel."
     Melos, XXV, (Oct. 1958), 320.

520. ------ and ------ "Klangumwandlungen durch Frequen-
     zumsetzung." _Gravesaner Blätter_, 4 (May 1956),
     35.

521. Heckman, D. "The new iconoclasts; a discussion of
     the recorded work of avant garde classical compo-
     sers." _Down Beat_, XXX (Feb. 14, 1963), 18.

522. Heckmann, Harald. "Neue Methoden der Verarbeitung
     musikalischer Daten." _Die Musikforschung_, XVII,
     4 (1964), 381.

523. Heike, Georg. "Informationstheorie und musikalische
     Komposition." _Melos_, XXVIII, 9 (Sept. 1961),
     269.

524. Heinsheimer, Hans W. "Space music and music for the
     space age." _Portfolio and Art News Annual_, 2
     (1960), 104.

525. Heinze, B. "Musique concrète." _Canon_, VII (July
     1954), 516.

526. Heiss, Hermann. "Spezialaufnahmeaggregat für Ton-
     gemische"/"Record-playback head for tone mixtures."
     Gravesaner Blätter/Gravesano Review, IV, 15-16
     (1960), 118/123.

527. Helm, Everett. "As dead as C major." _The New York
     Times_, CX (May 14, 1961), section 2, 9.

528. ------ "Biennale 1961." _Musical America_, LXXXI
     (June 1961), 32.

529. ------ "Darmstadt International Holiday Courses for
     new music." _The Musical Quarterly_, XLV, 1 (Jan.
     1959), 100.

530. ------ "The dwindling racket." _High Fidelity_, X,
     8 (August 1960), 43.

531. ------ "The dilemma of avant garde music." The World of Music, IV, 6 (1962), 123.

532. ------ "Electronics and instrumental performance." The Instrumentalist, XIV (Dec. 1959), 34.

533. ------ "Experimentelle Musik in den USA." Melos, XXXI, 4 (April 1964), 123. Das Orchester, XII (June 1964), 208.

534. ------ "ISCM concert." Musical America, LXXXII (May 1962), 39.

535. ------ "Music in Yugoslavia." In Lang and Broder, eds., Contemporary music in Europe. New York, G. Schirmer, 1965, 215. The Musical Quarterly, LI, 1 (Jan. 1965), 215.

536. ------ "Space music in Venice." The Music Review, XXII (August 1961), 229.

537. "Helsinki: Erik Tawaststjerna founding electronic studio." World of Music, IV, 3 (June 1962), 56.

538. Hemsath, William. See Wilding-White, Raymond.

539. Henahan, D.J. "Comments on classics" (computer composition). Down Beat, XXX, 10 (April 23, 1964), 33.

540. Henderson, R. "Berio." The Musical Times, CV (April 1964), 278.

541. ------ "Stabiles, mobiles, & musikalische Graphik." The Musical Times, CV (April 1964), 288.

542. Henry, Otto W. "A preliminary checklist: books and articles on electronic music." New Orleans, Tulane University, Newcomb College Electronic Music Studio, June 1966 (mimeograph).

543. Henze, Hans Werner. "Wo stehen wir heute?" Darmstädter Beiträge zur neuen Musik, I (1958).

544. Herzfeld, Friedrich. "Homunkulus." In Musica Nova. Berlin, Ullstein, 1954, 309.

545. Hijman, J. "Elektronisch Componeren?" Mens en Melodie, XVI (May 1961), 141.

546. Hiller, Lejaren A., Jr. "Acoustics and electronic music in the university music curriculum." American Music Teacher, XII, 4 (1963), 24.

547. ------ "Computer Music." Scientific American, CCI, 6 (Dec. 1959), 109.

548. ------ "Electronic and computer music." St. Louis Post-Dispatch, LXXXI, 136 (May 17, 1959), music section, 50.

549. ------ "Electronic music at the University of Illinois." Journal of Music Theory, VII, 1 (Spring 1963), 99.

550. ------ "The electrons go around and come out music." Institute of Radio Engineers Student Quarterly, VIII, 1 (Sept. 1961), 37.

551. ------ "Information theory and musical analysis." Urbana, University of Illinois Experimental Music Studio, Technical Report No. 5, July 1962 (mimeograph).

552. ------ "Informationstheorie und Musik." Darmstädter Beiträge zur neuen Musik, VIII (1964), 7.

553. ------ "Instruction manual for sound generation by means of the CSX-1 Computer." Urbana, University of Illinois Experimental Music Studio, Technical Report No. 11, June 1965 (mimeograph).

554. ------ "An integrated electronic music console." Journal of the Audio Engineering Society, XIII, 2 (April 1965), 142.

555. ------ "Jüngste Entwicklung auf dem Gebiet der Computermusik." Darmstädter Beiträge zur neuen Musik, VIII (1964), 35.

556. ------ "Musikalische Andwendungen von elektronischen Digitalrechnern"/"Musical applications of electronic digital computers." Gravesaner Blätter/

<u>Gravesano Review</u>, 27-28 (Nov. 1965), 46/62.

557. ------ "Musique électronique." <u>In Encyclopédie des</u>
<u>sciences modernes</u>, VIII. Geneva, Kister, 1958, 110.

558. ------ "Muzyczne zastosowanie elektronowych maszyn
cyfrowych." <u>Ruch Muzyczny</u>, VI, 7 (April 1962),
11.

559. ------ "Report on contemporary experimental music,
1961." Urbana, University of Illinois Experimental Studio, Technical Report No. 4, June 1962.

560. ------ "A review of Decca recording DL-9103, 'Music
from mathematics.'" <u>Proceedings of the Institute</u>
<u>of Electronic and Electrical Engineers</u>, LI, 3
(March 1963), 538.

561. ------ "Some structural principles of computer music." <u>Journal of the American Musicological Soci-</u>
<u>ety</u>, IX, 3 (Fall 1956), 247.

562. ------ See Bode, Harald.

563. ------ and Robert A. Baker. "Computer cantata."
Urbana, University of Illinois Experimental Music Studio, Technical Report No. 8, Oct. 1963
(mimeograph).

564. ------ and ------ "<u>Computer Cantata</u>: a study in
compostional method." <u>Perspectives of New Music</u>,
III, 1 (Fall-Winter 1964), 62.

565. ------ and ------ "Computer music." Chapter 18 in
Borko, ed., <u>Computer applications in the behavioral</u>
<u>sciences</u>. Englewood Cliffs, N.J., Prentice-Hall,
1962, 424.

566. ------ and James Beauchamp. "Research in music with
electronics." <u>Science</u>, CL (Oct. 8, 1965), 161.

567. ------ and Leonard M. Isaacson. <u>Experimental music</u>.
New York, McGraw-Hill, 1959.

568. ------ and ------ <u>Experimental music</u>. Reviewed in
<u>The Music Review</u>, XXII, 4 (Nov. 1961), 326.

569. ------ and ------ Experimental music. Reviewed in
     Slovenská Hudba, VIII, 4 (1964), 128.

570. ------ and ------ "Experimental music." Chapter
     3 in Sayre and Crosson, eds., The modeling of
     mind -- computers and intelligence. Notre Dame,
     Indiana, University of Notre Dame Press, 1963,
     43.

571. ------ and ------ "Musical composition with a high
     speed digital computer." Journal of the Audio
     Engineering Society, VI, 3 (July 1958), 154.

572. Hirsch, N. "La neuve dans la bataille." Musica
     (Chaix), 119 (Feb. 1964), 11.

573. "Historique de la musique concrète." La Revue mu-
     sicale, 236 (1957), 137.

574. "Historique des recherches de musique concrète."
     La Revue musicale, 244 (1959), 57.

575. Hitchcock, H. Wiley. "Current chronicle: Ann Arbor,
     Michigan." The Musical Quarterly, XLVIII, 2 (April
     1962), 245.

576. ------ "Frontiers in music today." American Music
     Teacher, X, 6 (1961), 6.

577. Höchel, L. "Electronická ladicka a jeji pouziti ve
     vyzkumu a vede." Hudební Rozhledy, XVII, 6 (1964),
     256.

578. Hodeir, André. La musique depuis Debussy. Paris,
     Presses Universitaires de France, 1961. Trans-
     lated by N. Burch as Since Debussy: a view of
     contemporary music. New York, Grove Press, 1961.

579. Holde, Artur. "Electronic music synthesizer: ein
     Klangerzeuger." Das Musikleben, VIII (July-August
     1955), 263.

580. ------ "The electronic music synthesizer: Neue Medien
     der Klangerzeugung." Neue Zeitschrift für Musik,
     CXXI (Oct. 1960), 361.

581. Holford, F. "Music in Germany." <u>Canon</u>, XV (June 1962), 9.

582. Holloway, Jack E. "Electronic music." Köln, 1959 (mimeograph).

583. Holoch, G. "Elektronische Klangerzeugung nach dem Prinzip der Lichtpunktabtastung von Schablonen." <u>Nachrichtentechnische Fachberichte</u>, XV (1959).

584. Holt, J. Gordon. "On the compleat in fidelytie: a zany disc." <u>High Fidelity</u>, VI (April 1956), 88.

585. Hopkins, A.L., Jr. See Brooks, F.P., Jr.

586. Howe, Hubert S., Jr. "Music and electronics: a report." <u>Perspectives of New Music</u>, IV, 2 (Spring-Summer 1966), 68.

587. "How's Petrillo gonna collect AFM dues from RCA's electronic tooter?" <u>Variety</u>, CXCVII (Feb. 2, 1955), 55.

588. Hoyler, C.N. See Pike, W.S.

589. Hrusovsky, Ivan. "Do diskusie o experimente." <u>Slovenská Hudba</u>, VI (Jan. 1962), 18.

590. Huggins, Phyllis. "Three-part music with a computer as one part." <u>Computers and Automation</u>, VI, 3 (1958), 8.

591. Hughes, Allen. "Dance: created on stage." <u>The New York Times</u>, CXIV (July 25, 1965), 68.

592. Hunt, F.V. <u>Electroacoustics</u>. Cambridge, Mass., Harvard University Press, 1954.

593. Hürlimann, Martin. See Thienhaus, Erich.

594. Hurnik, I. "Rada jako sluzebnik a diktator." <u>Hudební Rozhledy</u>, XV, 3 (1962), 94.

595. Husemann, H. "Elektroakustische Glockengeläute." <u>Elektromeister</u>, XV, 5 (1962), 239.

596. "Inside stuff -- music (first 'stocastic work' composed by IBM coordinator 70.90)." Variety, CCVII
(July 11, 1962), 65.

597. "Les instruments de musique et l'électronique."
Musique et Radio, LII, 619 (Nov. 1962), 47.

598. "Interesting experiment." Musical Courier, CLIX
(March 1959), 41.

599. "International survey (in sound) of compositions
using tape resources" (abstract). Journal of the
Acoustical Society of America, XXIX (1957), 770.

600. "Inventar des Experimentalstudios Gravesano." Gravesaner Blätter, 4 (May 1956), 64.

601. Isaacson, Leonard M. See Hiller, Lejaren A., Jr.

602. "Ist das Musik?" Das Musikleben, VIII (Jan. 1955),
3.

603. "It may scratch, but the music is not for boring."
American Record Guide, XXX (Nov. 1963), 195.

604. "Italy" (electronic studio installed in Accademia
Filarmonica). Score, 20 (June 1957), 71.

605. Ivey, Jean Eichelberger. "Electronic music in Toronto." Kansas Music Review, XXVI, 5 (Oct.-Nov.
1964), 6.

606. Jacobson, Homer. "Information and the human ear."
Journal of the Acoustical Society of America,
XXIII, 4 (July 1951), 463.

607. Jarocinski, Stefan. "Polish music after World War
II." In Lang and Broder, eds., Contemporary mu-
sic in Europe. New York, G. Schirmer, 1965, 244.
The Musical Quarterly, LI, 1 (Jan. 1965), 244.

608. Jeanneret-Gris, Charles-Édouard (Le Corbusier).
Le Poème électronique. Paris, Editions de Minuit,
1958.

609. ------ L.C. Kalff, and Jean (Yannis) Xenakis.

"The Philips Pavilion and The Electronic Poem."
Arts and Architecture, LXXV, 11 (Nov. 1958), 23.

610. Jenny, G. "Initiation à la lutherie électronique."
Toute la radio, (Sept. 1955), 289; (Nov. 1955),
397; (Dec. 1955), 455; (Jan. 1956), 23; (Feb.
1956), 67.

611. Joachim, H. "Das Missverständnis von Pierre Schaeffer." *Melos*, XXI (May 1954), 140.

612. Joachim, Otto. "Books: Electronic Music." *Canadian
Music Journal*, III, 2 (Winter 1959), 75 (see 938).

613. John, R.W. "Recollections of David." *Educational
Music Magazine*, XXXV (Sept.-Oct. 1955), 18.

614. "Joseph Tal, composer." *Musical Courier*, CLVII,
6 (May 1958), 37.

615. Judd, Frederick C. "The composition of electronic
music." *Audio and Record Review*, 1 (Nov. 27,
1961).

616. ------ "Effects with a tape recorder." *The Radio
Constructor*, (June-July 1956).

617. ------ *Electronic music and music concrète*. London,
Neville Spearman, 1961.

618. ------ "Electronic music: sound sources and treat-
ment." *Wireless World*, LXVII (Sept. 1961), 483.
Annales des Télécommunications, 149253, 4 (1962).

619. ------ "Electronic sounds and music." *Practical
Electronics*, I, 12 (Oct. 1965), 838.

620. ------ "Manipulation of signals for musique concrète." *Tape Recording Magazine*, (Jan. 27, 1960).

621. ------ "Musique concrète." *Stereo Sound Magazine*,
(Aug. 1959).

622. ------ "Radiophonics at the B.B.C." *Amateur Tape
Recording, Video & Hi-Fi*, V, 10 (May 1964), 8.

623. Kaczynski, T. "Czyzby bezideowosc mlodziezy?" Ruch Muzyczny, VI, 20 (1962), 3.

624. "Kafka mit musique concrète im Staatstheater Kassel." Melos, XXII (July-August 1955), 222.

625. Kagel, Mauricio. "Det instrumentale teater." Dansk Musiktidsskrift, XXXVII, 7 (1962), 221.

626. —————— "Om tilhørerens visuelle oplevelse." Dansk Musiktidsskrift, XXXIX, 4 (1964), 111.

627. —————— "Ton-Cluster, Anschläge, Ubergänge"/"Tone-clusters, attacks, transitions." Die Reihe, V/5 (1959/1961), 23/40.

628. Kalff, L.C. See Jeanneret-Gris, Charles-Édouard.

629. Karkoschka, Erhard. Das Schriftbild der neuen Musik. Ceele, Moeck, 1966.

630. —————— "Stockhausens Theorien." Melos, XXXII, 1 (Jan. 1965), 5.

631. Kasan, Jaroslav. "Elektronische Musik in der CSSR." Music und Gesellschaft, XV (Feb. 1965), 124.

632. —————— "Elektronische Musik in der Tschechoslowakei." Musica, XVIII, 6 (1964), 320. "Muzyka elektronowa w Czechoslowacji." Ruch Muzyczny, VIII, 19 (1964), 12. In English: Musical Events, (Aug. 1964).

633. Kasemets, Udo. "Current Chronicle: Ann Arbor." The Musical Quarterly, L, 4 (Oct. 1964), 515.

634. —————— See Beckwith, John.

635. Katz, L. "Simulating piano tones electronically." Electronics, XXVI (Oct. 1953), 155.

636. Kelin, H. "Klangsynthese und Klanganalyse im elektronischen Studio." Frequenz, XVI, 3 (March 1962), 109. Annales des Télécommunications, 155876, 12 (1962).

637. Keller, Wilhelm. "Elektronische Musik und Musique

concrète." <u>Merkur</u>, IX (Sept. 1955), 877.

638. Kelly, Warren E. "Tape music composition for secondary school." <u>Music Educators Journal</u>, LII, 6 (June-July 1966), 86.

639. Kendall, Osmond. "Method and apparatus for producing sounds." Ottawa, The Patent Office, No. 542,589, June 25, 1957.

640. Kent, Earle Lewis. "Electronic music -- past, present, and future." <u>Transactions of the Institute of Radio Engineers</u>, AU-1 (March-April 1953), 1.

641. ------ "Electronic music box" (abstract). <u>Journal of the Acoustical Society of America</u>, XXIV (1952), 116.

642. ------ "Electronic music maker" (abstract). <u>Journal of the Acoustical Society of America</u>, XXIX (1957), 768.

643. ------ "A method for changing the frequency of a complex tone." Ann Arbor, University Microfilms No. 3518, 1951.

644. ------ and C.J. Tennes. "An electronic music box." <u>Proceedings of the National Electronics Conference</u>, VII (1951), 115. <u>Annales des Télécommunications</u>, VII, 50859 (Dec. 1952).

645. Kerr, Russell. "The nation's music: New York." <u>Musical Courier</u>, CLXIII (June 1961), 17.

646. Kirk, J. "Electronic musical novelty." <u>Radio-Television News</u>, XLIV (August 1950), 38.

647. Kisielewski, S. "Postep i przemijanie." <u>Ruch Muzyczny</u>, VIII, 11 (1964), 8.

648. Klaw, Spencer. "The cultural innovators." <u>Fortune</u>, LXI (Feb. 1960), 146.

649. Klebe, Giselher. "Erste praktische Arbeit"/"First practical work." <u>Die Reihe</u>, I/1 (1955/1958), 20/17.

650. Klein, H. "Elektronische Klanggestaltung mittels Lochstreifen." München, Siemens and Halske, Studio für Elektronische Musik.

651. ------ "Uber eine Apparatur zur Steuerung und Verformung von Klängen." Nachrichtentechnische Fachberichte, XV (1959).

652. Klein, Howard. "Music of the here and now." The New York Times, CXIV (July 18, 1965), X19.

653. Klein, M.S. "Uncommon uses for common digital computers." Instruments and Automation, XXX (Feb. 1957), 251.

654. Knudsen, Vern O. "Some cultural applications of modern acoustics." Journal of the Acoustical Society of America, IX, 3 (Jan. 1938), 175.

655. Kobold, H. "Lobt Gott mit elektrischen Summern!?" Musik und Kirche, XXIV (Nov.-Dec. 1954), 247.

656. Koch, P. "'Electronenschocks' -- auch ein Weg zur neuen Musik." Neue Zeitschrift für Musik, CXXV, 2 (1964), 67.

657. Koenig, Gottfried Michael. "Bo Nilsson." Die Reihe, IV/4 (1958/1960), 85.

658. ------ "Kommentar." Die Reihe, VIII (1962), 73.

659. ------ "Neue notationsformen." Musikhandel, XIII, 1 (1962), 5.

660. ------ "The second phase of electronic music." Utrecht, Rijksuniversiteit, Studio voor Elektronische Muziek, Summer 1965 (mimeograph).

661. ------ "Studiotechnik"/"Studio technique." Die Reihe, I/1 (1955/1958), 29/52.

662. ------ "Studium im Studio." Die Reihe, V/5 (1959/1961), 74/30.

663. ------ "Via Electronica." In Movens. Wiesbaden, Limes Verlag, 1960.

664. Kolben, Robert. "Zur Entwicklungsgeschichte des Stereophoners"/"The stereophoner." <u>Gravesaner Blätter/Gravesano Review</u>, IV, 13 (1959), 55/63.

665. Kondracki, Michal. "Edgar Varèse (1883-1965)." <u>Ruch Muzyczny</u>, IX, 24 (Jan. 15-31, 1966), 2.

666. ------ "List z USA." <u>Ruch Muzyczny</u>, V, 15 (1961), 13; VII, 15 (1963), 10.

667. Könnicke, Walter. "Zur neueren Entwicklung auf dem Gebiet der Elektrik-musik." <u>Instrumentenbau Zeitschrift</u>, VIII (1954), 268.

668. Kortsen, Bjarne. <u>Elektronisk musikk</u>. Haugesund, The Author, 1965.

669. Koster, Ernst. Article in <u>Rufer und Hörer</u>, VI (1952), 519.

670. ------ "Elektronische Musikinstrumente." <u>Das Musik-leben</u>, VII (1954), 128.

671. ------ "Kinderkrankheiten der elektrogenen Musik." <u>Musica</u>, IX (July 1955), 315.

672. ------ "Konkrete Musik zum Tanz." <u>Musica</u>, XIII (Oct. 1959), 639.

673. Kotschenreuther, Hellmut. Article in <u>Musikstadt Berlin</u>. Berlin, Bote und Bock, 1958.

674. Křenek, Ernst. "Den Jüngeren über die Schulter ge-schaut"/"A glance over the shoulders of the young." <u>Die Reihe</u>, I/1 (1955/1958), 31/14.

675. ------ "Lydteorier; betragtninger over elektron-Musik." <u>Dansk Musiktidsskrift</u>, XXXII (May 1957), 31.

676. ------ "New development in electronic music." <u>Musical America</u>, LXXV (Sept. 1955), 8.

677. ------ "Tradition in perspective." <u>Perspectives of New Music</u>, I, 1 (Fall 1962), 27.

578. ------ "Zur Geheimsprache der modernen Musiklitera-
tur." _Musica_, XVIII, 6 (Nov.-Dec. 1964), 287.

579. ------ _Zur Sprache gebracht_. München, Langen und
Müller, 1958, 361.

580. Kristof, K. "Budapest buffoonery." _Opera News_,
XXVIII (Sept. 28, 1963), 27.

581. Krokover, R. "Music and dance." _Dance Magazine_,
XXXV (August 1961), 24.

682. Kučera, V. "Technika a hudba." _Hudební Rozhledy_,
XVI, 9 (1963), 385.

583. Kuttner, Fritz A. "Musicologist reveals his affair
with Susie." _HiFi/Stereo Review_, XV, 3 (Sept.
1965), 54.

684. Kux, Ralph. "Elektronische Musik." _Goethe_, XXXIV
(1955), 337.

685. Kwasnik, Walter. "Aesthetic and playability require-
ments of electronic organs." Ottawa, National
Research Council of Canada, Technical Translation
TT-627, 1956 (translation of 688).

686. ------ "Elektronische Musikinstrumente." _Technische
Mitteilungen_, XLVI, 12 (1953), 416.

687. ------ "Erfolge und neue Ziele im Bau elektronischer
Musikinstrumente." _Instrumentenbau Zeitshcrift_,
VIII (1954), 166.

688. ------ "Klangästhetische und spieltechnische Erfor-
dernisse bei Elektronen-Orgeln." _Frequenz_, V
(1951), 27.

689. ------ "Marktfähige elektronische Musikinstrumente."
Feinwerktechnik, LIX, 3 (1955), 85.

690. Kyle, M.K. "AmerAllegro." _Pan Pipes_, LV, 2 (1963),
38; LVI, 2 (1964), 69.

691. Labroca, Mario, _et al_. "Un problema aperto." _La
Biennale_, XI, 44-45 (Dec. 1961), 3.

692. Laible, U. "Musikinstrumentenbau und Elektronik."
     Musikhandel, XV (Sept. 1964), 323.

693. Lamare, Jean-Yves. "La musique concrète est-elle
     musicale?" **Guide du concert**, XXXIX (June 5, 1959),
     116.

694. Lamb, H. "'The avant gardist,' a product of prog-
     ress." **Music Journal**, XXII (Jan. 1964), 22.

695. Lang, Paul Henry. "Editorial." **The Musical Quar-
     terly**, XLVI, 2 (April 1960), 145. Appears as
     "Introduction," in Lang, ed. **Problems of modern
     music**. New York, W.W. Norton, 1962, 1.

696. ------ "Introduction." In Lang and Broder, eds.,
     Contemporary music in Europe. New York, G. Schir-
     mer, 1965, 1. **The Musical Quarterly**, LI, 1
     (Jan. 1965), 1.

697. ------ ed. **Problems of modern music**. New York, W.W.
     Norton, 1962. Appeared originally as **The Musical
     Quarterly**, XLVI, 2 (April 1960).

698. ------ and Nathan Broder, eds. **Contemporary music
     in Europe**. New York, G. Schirmer, 1965. Appeared
     originally as **The Musical Quarterly**, LI, 1 (Jan.
     1965).

699. Langer, Yvette. "Bibliographie sommaire de la
     musique mécanisée." **Polyphonie**, 6 (1950), 144.

700. Lapham, L.H. "Music for machines." **The Saturday
     Evening Post**, CCXXXVII (Jan. 18, 1964), 66.

701. La Prade, Ernest. "Electronic musical instruments."
     In Willi Apel, ed., **Harvard Dictionary of Music**.
     Cambridge, Harvard University Press, 1956, 235.

702. Larner, G. "Recherche." **Musical Opinion**, LXXXI
     (March 1958), 385.

703. Larson, C. "A new world for music; from an inter-
     view with Harry F. Olson." **Etude**, LXXIV (May-
     June 1956), 19.

704. La Rue, Jan. "An electronic concert in New York." *The Music Review*, XXII, 3 (1961), 223.

705. ------ "Two electronic seminars at Yale." *The Music Review*, XXIII, 2 (1962), 140.

706. Lawrence, Harold. "The composing machine." *Audio*, XXXIX (April 1955), 10.

707. ------ "Electronic music, home style." *Audio*, XLV (May 1961), 70.

708. ------ "Electronics by leaps and bounds." *Audio*, XLV (May 1961), 70.

709. ------ "Is 'live' music on the way out?" *Audio Engineering*, XXVIII (Sept. 1954), 14.

710. ------ "The loneliness of the electronic composer." *Audio*, L (July 1966), 50.

711. ------ "Music criticism in the electronic age." *Audio*, XLIV (Oct. 1960), 78.

712. ------ "Of mikes and men -- John Cage again." *Audio*, XLVII, 11 (Nov. 1963), 64.

713. ------ "Music in the laboratory." *Audio*, XLI (Jan. 1957), 52.

714. ------ "Splitting the tone." *Audio*, XLI (Nov. 1957), 78.

715. Lébl, Vladimír. *Elektronická Hudba*. Praha, Státní Hudební Vydavatelství, 1966.

716. Le Caine, Hugh. "Electronic music." *Proceedings of the Institute of Radio Engineers*, XLIV (April 1956), 457. A different text with this title appears in *New Scientist*, XXVIII, 473 (Dec. 16, 1965), 814.

717. ------ "From the labs: a new music." *The Financial Post* (Toronto), L, 39 (Sept. 29, 1956), 52.

718. ------ "Revised specification for a tape recorder for use in electronic music studios developed by the National Research Council of Canada." Ottawa,

National Research Council of Canada, Radio and
Electrical Engineering Division, ERB-581, May 1961.

719. ------ "Synthetic means." In Beckwith and Kasemets,
eds., The modern composer and his world. Toronto,
University of Toronto Press, 1961, 109.

720. ------ "A tape recorder for use in electronic music
studios and related equipment." Journal of Music
Theory, VII, 1 (Spring 1963), 83. Ottawa, National
Research Council of Canada, 7467, 1963.

721. ------ "A touch-sensitive keyboard for the organ."
The Canadian Music Journal, III, 3 (Spring 1959),
26.

722. ------ "Touch-sensitive organ based on an electro-
static coupling device." Journal of the Acoustical
Society of America, XXVII, 4 (July 1955), 781.

723. ------ and John M. Bowsher. "Tape-recorder for cre-
ative use in an electronic music studio" (abstract).
Journal of the Acoustical Society of America, XXXI
(1959), 839.

724. Leeuw, Ton de. "Elektronische Probleme in den
Niederlanden." Melos, XXX (May 1963), 161.

725. ------ Experimentele muziek. Hilversum, Avro, 1958.

726. Leitner, P. Logische Programme für automatische
Musik. Wien, Staatsprüfungsarbeit an der Technischen Hochschule, 1957.

727. Leonard, L. "Is musique concrète an art form?"
Musical Opinion, LXXVIII (Nov. 1954), 87.

728. Levinson, L.L. "'No Exit' track with Viveca Lind-
fors rescues electronic music recital." Variety,
CCXXX (May 22, 1963), 56.

729. Lewer, S.K. Electronic musical instruments. London,
Electronic Engineering, 1948.

730. ------ Electronic musical instruments. Reviewed
in Journal of the Acoustical Society of America,

XX (April, 1949), 97.

731. ------ "The future of electronic music." Electronic Engineering, XVII (June 1944), 32. Wireless Engineer, XXI (1944), abstract 3894.

732. Lewinski, Wolf-Eberhard von. "Current chronicle: Germany." The Musical Quarterly, LII, 3 (July 1966), 376.

733. ------ "Das elektronische Studio von Hermann Heiss." Melos, XXVII (Nov. 1960), 351.

734. ------ "Junge Komponisten"/"Young composers." Die Reihe, IV/4 (1958/1960), 5/1.

735. ------ "Kompositorische Spiele mit Klang und Farbe bei Radio Bremen." Melos, XXVIII, 10 (Oct. 1961), 322.

736. ------ "Eine Messe mit elektronische Mitteln" (Hermann Heiss). Melos, XXXI (June 1964), 173.

737. ------ "Phantasie und Effekt in Darmstadt." Melos, XXIX (Oct. 1962), 329.

738. ------ "The variety of trends in modern German music." In Lang and Broder, eds., Contemporary music in Europe. New York, G. Schirmer, 1965, 166. The Musical Quarterly, LI, 1 (Jan. 1965), 166.

739. Lewis, R.E. and Norman McLaren. "'End of the world': 'radiophonic' music play." Journal of the Society of Motion Picture and Television Engineers, LX (March 1958).

740. ------ "Synthetic sound on film." Journal of the Society of Motion Picture Engineers, L (1948), 233.

741. Lietti, Alfredo. "Evolution des moyens techniques de la musique électronique." Revue Belge de Musicologie, XIII, 1-4 (1959), 40.

742. ------ "I fenomeni acustici aleatori nella musica

elettronica." <u>Incontri musicale</u>, 3 (1959), 150.

743. ------- "La scomposizione analitica del suono."
     <u>Incontri musicale</u>, 2 (1958).

744. ------- "Gli impianti tecnici dello studio di fono-
     logia musicale di Radio Milano." <u>Elettronica</u>,
     V, 3 (Sept. 1956), 116.

745. ------- "Soppressore di disturbi a selezione d'ampi-
     ezza." <u>Elettronica</u>, V (Sept.-Oct. 1955), 1.

746. ------- "The technical equipment of the electronic
     music studio of Radio Milano." Ottawa, National
     Research Council of Canada, Technical Translation
     TT-859, 1957 (translation of 744).

747. Lilien, I. "Sonie anno 1914: l'Arte dei Rumori van
     Luigi Russolo." <u>Mens en Melodie</u>, XVIII (July
     1963), 203.

748. Lima, Manuel de. "A música electrónica e a escola
     de Colonia." <u>Arte Musical</u>, XXVIII (Feb. 1959),
     107.

749. Limmert, Erich. "Hannover tanzt elektronisch."
     <u>Melos</u>, XXVI (Jan. 1959), 17.

750. Lin, Ehr. "Wir spielen auf der Rechenanlage"/"Play-
     ing the computer." <u>Gravesaner Blätter/Gravesano
     Review</u>, 27-28 (Nov. 1965), 73/81.

751. Lindlar, Heinrich. "Elektronische Musik im Kölner
     Funkhaus." <u>Melos</u>, XXI (Nov. 1954), 326.

752. ------ "Karlheinz Stockhausen." <u>Die Musik in Ges-
     chichte und Gegenwart</u>, XII. Kassel, Bärenreiter,
     1965, 1368.

753. Lissa, Zofia. "'Konkrete' und elektronische Musik
     im Film." In <u>Aesthetik der Filmmusik</u>. Berlin,
     Henschelverlag, 1965, 292.

754. "Liste des oeuvres de musique concrète." <u>La Revue
     musicale</u>, 236 (1957), 139.

755. Lloyd, Kate. " ... and one evening when listeners 'floated away.'" <u>Vogue</u>, CXLVII, 9 (May 1966), 198.

756. "Locals advised regarding recent electronics devices (particularly the so-called 'side man')." <u>International Musician</u>, LIX (Jan. 1961), 7.

757. Loescher, F.A. "Technisches von der Tagung 'Fünf Jahre Gravesano'"/"Technical aspects at the fifth anniversary of Gravesano." <u>Gravesaner Blätter/ Gravesano Review</u>, IV, 15-16 (1960), 5/12.

758. Logan, B.F. See Schroeder, M.R.

759. Lohmüller, Helmut. "München fördert die elektronische Musik." <u>Melos</u>, XXXI, 12 (Dec. 1964), 405.

760. ------ "München ist ein Umschlagplatz für zeitgenössische Musik." <u>Melos</u>, XXXIII, 9 (Sept. 1966), 281.

761. "'Look, Ma, no sidemen' with RCA's music synthesizer bow on wax." <u>Variety</u>, CXCIX (Feb. 2, 1955), 55.

762. Lord, Arthur. See Martin, Constant.

763. Lottermoser, Werner. "Akustische Beurteilung elektronischer Musikinstrumente." <u>Archiv für Musikwissenschaft</u>, XII, 4 (1955), 249.

764. Lowe, J. "Tape recorder spurs new interests for audio-minded home owners." <u>Musical America</u>, LXXV (March 1955), 21.

765. "Luciano Berio." <u>Santa Cecilia</u>, XI (April 1962), 43.

766. Ludden, Bennet. "Composing music by the yard." <u>Musical Courier</u>, CXLIX (Jan. 1, 1954), 6.

767. Luening, Otto C. "American tape music, past, present and future" (abstract). <u>Journal of the Acoustical Society of America</u>, XXVI (1954), 944.

768. ------ "Electronic music: a practical guide." <u>Music</u>

Today, III, 1 (Nov.-Dec. 1960), 3.

769. ------ "Karlheinz Stockhausen." Juilliard Review, VI (Winter 1958-1959), 10.

770. ------ "New sound techniques in music." In Art and Artist. Berkeley, University of California Press, 1962.

771. ------ "Relationship of new sound materials to compositional techniques in music" (abstract). Journal of the Acoustical Society of America, XXIX (1957), 770.

772. ------ "Some random remarks about electronic music." Journal of Music Theory, VIII, 1 (1964), 89.

773. ------ See Prieberg, Fred K.

774. "Luening-Ussachevsky tape work premièred." Musical America, LXXV (Dec. 15, 1955), 21.

775. Lyon, Raymond. "'Algorithme I,' musique écrit par une machine pour le film 'Imprévisibles.'" Guide du concert, 330 (Nov. 17, 1961), 385.

776. ------ "La musique algorithmique." Guide du concert, 336 (Jan. 12, 1962), 610.

777. ------ "Musique expérimentale: UNESCO concert." Guide du concert, 210 (Nov. 14, 1958), 313.

778. MacDermott, Vincent. "Current chronicle: The Netherlands." The Musical Quarterly, LII, 4 (Oct. 1966), 511.

779. MacDonald, Neil. "Music by automatic computers." Computers and Automation, VII, 3 (1958), 8.

780. Mâche, François-Bernard. "Connaissance des structures sonores." La Revue musicale, 244 (1959), 17.

781. ------ "Einige 'konkrete' Probleme der elektronischen Musik"/"Some 'concrete' problems." Gravesaner Blätter/Gravesano Review, 27-28 (Nov. 1965), 107/

782. ------ "Le réalisme en musique." Situation de la recherche, Cahiers d'études de radio-télévision, 27-28 (Sept.-Dec. 1960), 63. Paris, Flammarion.

783. ------ "Le référendum." La Revue musicale, 247 (June 1959), 6.

784. Macfadyen, K.A. Article in The Radio and Electronic Engineer, XXVII (1964), 365.

785. "The machine closes in." Time, LXXIX, 7 (Feb. 16, 1962), 65.

786. Machlis, Joseph. "Electronic music." In Introduction to contemporary music. New York, W.W. Norton, 1961, 425.

787. MacLow, Jackson. See Young, La Monte.

788. "Macnagten concerts." Musical Opinion, LXXXIV, 999 (Dec. 1960), 143.

789. Mager, Jörg. Eine neue Epoche der Musik durch Radio. Berlin, 1924.

790. "Das Magnetofon -- ein neues Musikinstrument?" Neue Zeitschrift für Musik, CXVIII (March 1957), 193.

791. Malik, Miroslaw. "O psychofyziologickem účinu elektronické hudby." Hudební Rozhledy, XVIII, 5 (1965), 184.

792. Mann, Michael. "Reaction and continuity in musical composition." The Music Review, XV (Feb. 1959), 39.

793. Manzoni, Giacomo. "Breve introduzione alla musica elettronica." La Rassegna musicale, XXVII (Dec. 1957), 309.

794. Maren, Roger. "Electronic music: untouched by human hands." The Reporter, XVI (April 18, 1957), 40.

795. ------ "Music by montage and mixing." The Reporter, XIII (Oct. 6, 1955), 38.

796. ------ "Music untouched by human hands." Science Digest, XLII (August 1957), 29.

797. Marie, Jean-Étienne. "Musique électronique, expérimentale et concrète." In Alexis Roland-Manuel, ed., Histoire de la musique Pléiade, II. Paris, 1963, 1418.

798. ------ Musique vivante. Paris, 1953.

799. Marks, Robert. "Theremin plans electrical orchestra." Musical America, XLVIII (Sept. 15, 1928), 25.

800. Marlens, William S. "Duration and/or frequency alteration." Audio Engineering Society Preprint No. 412, 1965.

801. Marquis, George Welton. Twentieth century music idioms. Englewood Cliffs, N.J., Prentice-Hall, 1964.

802. "Marta Sanchez y sus experimentos con 'cerebros electrónicos.'" Revista Musical Chilena, XIV, 72 (1960), 143.

803. Martenot, Maurice. "Développement et application practique de l'Expérience de Melde." Électronique, L (Jan. 1951), 21. Annales des Télécommunications, VI, 36596 (March 1951).

804. ------ "Lutherie électronique." In La musique et ses problèmes contemporains 1953-1963. Paris, René Juilliard (Cahiers de la Compagnie Madeleine Renaud -- Jean-Louis Barrault, 41), 1963, 77.

805. Martin, Constant. "Instruments de musique électronique." Revue du son, 25 (May 1955), 177. Annales des Télécommunications, 76085 (July-August 1955).

806. ------ La musique électronique. Paris, Éditions Techniques et Vulgarisation, 1950.

807. ------ "The recent progress of electronic music."
The Organ, XXX, 120 (April 1951), 198. Replies
by Stanley L. Miller, R.H. Middleditch, and Arthur
Lord in The Organ, XXXI, 122 (Oct. 1951), 88.

808. Martin, D. "Acoustics and the arts." Sound -- Its
Uses and Control, II, 1 (1963), 28.

809. Martin, D.W. See Dorf, Richard H.

810. Martin, Vernon. "Bibliography of writings on electronic music." New York, Columbia-Princeton Electronic Music Center, 1964 (mimeograph).

811. Mathews, Max V. "An acoustic compiler for music and
psychological stimuli." Bell System Technical
Journal, XL, 3 (May 1961), 677.

812. ------ "Computer program to generate acoustic signals" (abstract). Journal of the Acoustical Society of America, XXXII (1960), 1493.

813. ------ "The digital computer as a musical instrument." Science, CXLII, 3592 (Nov. 1, 1963), 553.

814. ------ "Immediate sound generation" (abstract).
Journal of the Acoustical Society of America,
XXXIX, 6 (June 1966), 1245.

815. ------ "Schallplattenbeilage: Computermusik"/"The
computer music record supplement." Gravesaner
Blätter/Gravesano Review, VII, 26 (1965).

816. ------ See Pierce, John R.

817. ------ and N. Guttman. "Generation of music by a
digital computer." Proceedings of the Third International Congress on Acoustics, Stuttgart, 1959.
Amsterdam, Elsever Publishing Co., 253.

818. ------ and Joan E. Miller. "Computer program for
automatic composition and generation of music"
(abstract). Journal of the Acoustical Society
of America, XXXV (1963), 1908.

819. ------ and ------ Music IV programmer's manual.

Murray Hill, N.J., Bell Telephone Laboratories, 1965.

820. ------, John R. Pierce and N. Guttman. "Musikalische Klänge von Digitalrechnern"/"Musical sounds from digital computers." <u>Gravesaner Blätter/Gravesano Review</u>, VI, 23-24 (1962), 109/119.

821. ------, ------, and ------ "The sound of music from digital computers." <u>Institute of Electronic and Electrical Engineers Student Journal</u>, I, 4 (Sept. 1963), 25.

822. Matthews, John. "The Scapegoat, score by Bülent Arel of Ankara." <u>Educational Theatre Journal</u>, XIII, 2 (May 1961), 146.

823. Matzke, Hermann. "Musique concrète. Instrumental-musik ohne Musikinstrumente." <u>Instrumentenbau Zeitschrift</u>, VIII (1953), 22.

824. ------ "Wo steht die elektronische Musik heute?" <u>Instrumentenbau Zeitschrift</u>, IX (1955), 177.

825. ------ "Zur notwendige Vorbemerkungen zu einen leicht missverstandenen Thema." <u>Instrumentenbau Zeitschrift</u>, VIII (1954), 165.

826. Mauzey, Peter. "A control console for multi-speaker presentations of electronic music." <u>Journal of the Audio Engineering Society</u>, X, 4 (Oct. 1962), 338.

827. Mayer, H. "Musikale grafica (actieschrift)." <u>Mens en Melodie</u>, XIX (Sept. 1964), 276.

828. McLaren, Norman. "Synthesis of sound on film" (abstract). <u>Journal of the Acoustical Society of America</u>, XXXI (1959), 839.

829. ------ See Lewis, R.E.

830. "McMillan Academic Theatre." <u>Music Journal</u>, XXIII (Jan. 1965), 100.

831. "Mechanized music." <u>Musical America</u>, LXXX (Aug.

1960), 22.

832. Meinel, H. von. "Musikinstrumentenstimmungen und Tonsysteme." <u>Acustica</u>, VII (1957), 185.

833. Mellers, Wilfred H. "The avant-garde in America." <u>Proceedings of the Royal Musical Association</u>, XC (1963-1964), 1.

834. Meninger, Milan. "Znovu o psychofyziologickem účinu elektronické hudby." <u>Hudební Rozhledy</u>, XVIII, 8 (1965), 319.

835. Messiaen, Olivier. "Preface." <u>La Revue musicale</u>, 244 (1959), 5.

836. Metzger, Heinz-Klaus. "Gescheiterte Begriffe in Theorie und Kritik der Musik"/"Abortive concepts in the theory and criticism of music." <u>Die Reihe</u>, V/5 (1959/1961), 41/21.

837. ------ "Intermezzo I"/"Intermezzo I (Just who is growing old?)." <u>Die Reihe</u>, IV/4 (1958/1960), 64/63.

838. ------ "Nochmals 'Wider die Natur.'" <u>Neue Zeitschrift für Musik</u>, CXVIII (May 1957), 329.

839. ------ "Vokal, instrumental, elektronisch: neue Musik im Kölner Funkhaus." <u>Melos</u>, XXIII (July-August 1956), 221.

840. "México: Conferencia de Carlos Jimenez Mabarak, sobre la Música Concreta." <u>Boletín Interamericano de Música</u>, 2 (Nov. 1957), 46.

841. Meyer, Leonard B. "Art by accident." <u>Horizon</u>, III (Sept. 1960), 1.

842. ------ "The end of the renaissance?" <u>The Hudson Review</u>, XVI, 2 (Summer 1963), 169.

843. Meyer-Denkmann, G. "Elektronik und Experimentalfilme ziehen auch in Bremen." <u>Melos</u>, XXXI (Oct. 1964), 310.

844. Meyer-Eppler, Werner. Elektrische Klangerzeugung.
Bonn, Ferd. Dümmler, 1949.

845. ------ Elektrische Klangerzeugung. Reviewed in
Zeitschrift für Musik, CXIII (Feb. 1952), 102.

846. ------ "Elektronische Kompositionstechnik." Melos,
XX, 1 (Jan. 1953), 5.

847. ------ "Elektronische Musik." In Winckel, ed.,
Klangstruktur der Musik. Berlin, Verlag für Radio-
Foto-Kinotechnik, 1955, 133.

848. ------ "Elektronische Musik: Gestaltungsmöglichkei-
ten. Notation, technische Einrichtungen." Deutsche
Universitäts-Zeitung, IX (Dec. 6, 1954), 9.

849. ------ Grundlagen und Anwendungen der Informationstheorie. Frankfurt, Springer-Verlag, 1959.

850. ------ "Informationstheoretische Probleme der musikalischen Kommunication." Revue Belge de Musicologie, XIII, 1-4 (1959), 44. Die Reihe, VIII (1962),
7. Gravesaner Blätter, VII, 26 (1965), 93. "Musical communication as a problem of information theory." Gravesano Review, VII, 26 (1965), 98.

851. ------ "Klangexperimente." In Bericht über 1951 Ton-
meistertagung Detmold Musik Akademie.

852. ------ "Kurzen Bericht über den Internationalen
Kongress 'Musik und Elektroakustik' in Gravesano."
Acustica, IV, 6 (1954), 680.

853. ------ "Leichte Musik und Elektrotechnik in Ver-
gangenheit und Gegenwart." Gravesaner Blätter,
2-3 (Jan. 1956), 76.

854. ------ "The mathematic-acoustical fundamentals of
electrical sound composition." Ottawa, National
Research Council of Canada, Technical Translation
TT-608, 1956 (translation of 855).

855. ------ "Mathematisch-akustische Grundlagen der elektrischen Klang-Komposition." Technische Hausmitteilungen des Nordwestdeutschen Rundfunks, VI, 1-2

(1954), 29. "Fondamenti acustico-matematici della composizione elettrica dei suoni." Elettronica, V, 3 (Sept. 1956), 123.

856. ------ "Principios de la música electrónica." Revista Musical Chilena, XIII, 64 (March-April 1959), 6 (translated by José Vicente Asuar).

857. ------ "Sichtbar gemachte Musik." Gravesaner Blätter, 1 (July 1955), 27.

858. ------ "Some problems of reproduction and perception of electronic tape music" (abstract). Journal of the Acoustical Society of America, XXVIII (1956), 791.

859. ------ "Statistische und psychologische Klangprobleme"/"Statistic and psychologic problems of sound." Die Reihe, I/1 (1955/1958), 22/55.

860. ------ "The terminology of electronic music." Ottawa, National Research Council of Canada, Technical Translation TT-602, 1956 (translation of 864).

861. ------ "Über die Anwendung elektronischer Klangmittel im Rundfunk." Technische Hausmitteilungen des Nordwestdeutschen Rundfunks, IV, 7-8 (1952), 130.

862. ------ "Welche Möglichkeiten behesten für eine sinnvolle Anwendung elektronischer Musikinstrumente?" In Proceedings of the ICA Congress on Electroacoustics. Delft, 1953, 239.

863. ------ "Wie lassen sich Klänge und Geräusche in Film und Rundfunk 'elektronisch' gestalten?" Die Umschau in Wissenschaft und Technik, III (1954), 81.

864. ------ "Zur Terminologie der elektronischen Musik." Technische Hausmitteilungen des Nordwestdeutschen Rundfunks, VI, 1-2 (1954), 5.

865. ------ ed. Gravesano: Musik, Raumgestaltung, Elektroakustik. Mainz, Arsviva Verlag, 1955.

866. ------ ed. Gravesano. Reviewed by Kurt H. Haase in Journal of the Acoustical Society of America XXI (1957), 398.

867. ------ ed. <u>Gravesano</u>. Reviewed by E. Skudrzyk in
    <u>Journal of the Acoustical Society of America</u>,
    XXVIII (1956), 996.

868. ------, H. Sendhoff, and R. Rupprath. "Residualton
    und Formantton (mit einer illustrierendem Schall-
    platte)"/"Residual tone and formant tone (with re-
    corded examples)." <u>Gravesaner Blätter/Gravesano
    Review</u>, IV, 14 (1959), 70/84.

869. Meyers, Robert G. "Technical bases of electronic
    music." <u>Journal of Music Theory</u>, VIII, 1 (Spring
    1964), 2; 2 (Winter 1964), 184.

870. Middleditch, R.H. See Martin, Constant.

871. Miessner, B.V. "Electronic music and instruments."
    <u>Proceedings of the Institute of Radio Engineers</u>,
    XXIV (1936), 1427.

872. Miessner, Benjamin Franklin. Letter ("Touch sen-
    sitive keying devices"). <u>Journal of the Acousti-
    cal Society of America</u>, XXVII (1955), 1227.

873. Migot, Georges. "De la nécessité technique et es-
    thétique de faire entendre des oeuvres de siècles
    lointains." <u>Bulletin du Centre de Documentation
    de Musique Internationale</u>, 2 (Oct. 1951), 3.

874. Milhaud, Darius. "Étude poétique (Musikbeilage)."
    <u>Gravesaner Blätter</u>, 5 (August 1956), 9.

875. ------ "Konstruierte Musik." <u>Gravesaner Blätter</u>,
    5 (August 1956), 14.

876. "Milhaud, Frank Martin e a música contemporânea."
    <u>Gazeta Musicale</u>, X, 116-117 (1960), 137.

877. Miller, Joan E. See Mathews, Max V.

878. Miller, Stanley L. See Martin, Constant.

879. Milner, A. "The vocal element in melody." <u>The
    Musical Times</u>, XCVII (March 1956), 131.

880. Missal, J. "The fallacy of mathematical composi-

tional techniques." <u>American Music Teacher</u>, XII, 2 (1962), 25.

881. Moles, Abraham André. "An attempt to classify certain methods of acoustic preparation applied to the musical signal." Ottawa, National Research Council of Canada, Technical Translation TT-661, 1957 (translation of 888).

882. ------ "Aussichten des Elektronischen Instrumentariums"/"The prospects of electronic instrumentation." <u>Gravesaner Blätter/Gravesano Review</u>, IV, 15-16 (1960), 21/36.

883. ------ "Les bases de la jouissance musicale." <u>Gravesaner Blätter</u>, 2-3 (Jan. 1956), 48.

884. ------ "The characterization of sound objects by use of the level recorder in musical acoustics." <u>Acustica</u>, IV, 1 (1954), 241.

885. ------ "Classifiction d'une sonothèque par cartes perforées." <u>Revue du son</u>, XCI (1959).

886. ------ "Concrète (musique)." In <u>Larousse de la musique</u>, I. Paris, Librarie Larousse, 1957, 219.

887. ------ "Des machines a créer de la musique." <u>Atomes</u>, XIV, 159 (1959), 307. <u>Annales des Télécommunications</u>, 122444 (Dec. 1959).

888. ------ "Essai de classification de quelques méthodes de préparation sonore du signal musical." <u>Annales des Télécommunications</u>, IX, 7-8 (1954), 201. <u>Cahiers d'acoustique</u>, (Oct. 1954).

889. ------ "Essai de vocabulaire graphique international de l'acoustique musicale et l'électroacoustique." <u>Gravesaner Blätter</u>, 1 (July 1955), 46.

890. ------ "Etude et représentation de la note complexe en acoustique musicale." <u>Annales des Télécommunications</u>, VII, 11 (1952), 430. "Studium und Darstellung des komplexen Tones in der musikalischen Akustik." <u>Funk und Ton</u>, VI (June 1953), 277.

891. ------ "Gravesaner Studien, Elektronische Klänge"/
     "Electronic sounds." _Gravesaner Blätter/Gravesano
     Review_, IV, 13 (1959), 69/70.

892. ------ "Eine Informationstheorie der Musik." _Nach-
     richtentechnische Fachberichte_, III (July 1956),
     47. _Annales des Télécommunications_, 89677 (Jan.
     1957).

893. ------ "Informationstheorie und ästhetische Empfin-
     dung." _Gravesaner Blätter_, 6 (Dec. 1956), 3.

894. ------ "Instrumentation électronique et musiques
     expérimentales." _La Revue musicale_, 244 (1959),
     40.

895. ------ "Machines à musique." _La Revue musicale_,
     236 (1957), 115.

896. ------ "La musique algorithmique, première musique
     calculée." _Revue du son_, XCIII, 1 (Jan. 1961),
     28.

897. ------ "Musique électronique et expérimentale." In
     Norbert Dufourcq, ed., _Histoire de la musique_.
     Paris, Librarie Larousse, 1959, 588.

898. ------ "Musique, physiologie et psychologie." _Situ-
     ation de la recherche, Cahiers d'études de radio-
     télévision_, 27-28 (Sept.-Dec. 1960), 63. Paris,
     Flammarion.

899. ------ _Les musiques expérimentales_. Paris, Éditions
     du Cercle d'Art Contemporain, 1960.

900. ------ "Muzyka, maszyny, kompozytor." _Ruch Muzyczny_,
     VI, 17 (1962), 1.

901. ------ "Das neue Verhältnis zwischen Musik und Mathe-
     matik"/"The new relationship between music and
     mathematics." _Gravesaner Blätter/Gravesano Re-
     view_, VI, 23-24 (1962), 98/104.

902. ------ "Neuere Entwicklungen der Informationstheorie
     der Musik." _Beihefte der Tonmeistertagung Det-
     mold Musik Akademie_, Oct. 1960.

903. ------ "Perspectives de l'instrumentation électronique." _Revue Belge de Musicologie_, XIII, 1-4 (1959), 11.

904. ------ _Physique et technique du bruit_. Dunod, Paris, 1954.

905. ------ "A report to the Rockefeller Foundation on the present state of experimental music." New York (?), 1956 (mimeograph).

906. ------ "Some basic aspects of an information theory of music." _Journal of the Audio Engineering Society_, VI, 3 (July 1958), 183. _Annales des Télécommunications_, 118266 (August-Sept. 1959).

907. ------ "Structure physique du signal en acoustique microphonique." _Thèse Sciences_, (March 28, 1952).

908. ------ "La structure physique du signal musical." _Revue scientifique_, XCI, 3 (July-Dec. 1953), 277. _Annales des Télécommunications_, 78386 (Nov. 1955).

909. ------ _Théorie de l'information et perception esthétique_. Paris, Flammarion, 1959. Translated by Joel E. Cohen as _Information theory and aesthetic perception_. Urbana, University of Illinois Press, 1965.

910. ------ and Friedrich Trautwein. "Das elektroakustische Institut Hermann Scherchen." _Gravesaner Blätter_, 5 (August 1956), 51.

911. ------ and Vladimir A. Ussachevsky. "L'emploi du spectrographe acoustique et le problème de la partition en musique expérimentale." _Annales des Télécommunications_, XII, 9 (Sept. 1957), 299.

912. Montagu-Nathan, M. "Radio in retrospect." _Musical Opinion_, LXXVII, 918 (March 1954), 359.

913. Moog, Robert A. "Voltage controlled electronic music modules." _Journal of the Audio Engineering Society_, XIII, 3 (July 1965), 200.

914. ------ "A voltage controlled low-pass high-pass

filter for audio signal processing." Audio Engineering Society Preprint No. 413, 1965.

915. Moor, Paul. "Sinus tones with nuts and bolts." Harper's Magazine, CCXXV (Oct. 1962), 49.

916. Moroi, M. "Elektronische und konkrete Musik in Japan." Melos, XXIX (Feb. 1962), 49.

917. Moroni, S. "Un compositore elettronica de musica." Antenna, XXVII (August 1956), 372. Annales des Télécommunications, 87462 (Nov. 1956).

918. Moser, H.J. "Verrauschte Sensationen." Das Musikleben, VI (Sept. 1953), 306.

919. Mühne, H.G. "ANS -- ein neues elektronisches Musikinstrument." Musik und Gesellschaft, XIV (July 1964), 445.

920. Mumma, Gordon. "An electronic music studio for the independent composer." Journal of the Audio Engineering Society, XII, 3 (July 1964), 240.

921. ------ "What is a performance: how the idea of playing music is changing." Selmer Bandwagon, XIII, 5 (Nov. 1965), 12.

922. Münster, Clemens. "Konkrete Musik. Eine polemische Epistel." Hochland, XLIV (1952), 460.

923. Müry, Albert. "Basler Tagung für elektronische und konkrete Musik." Schweizerische Musikzeitung, XCV (1955), 312.

924. Murzin, Yevgeny. "ANS -- elektronnyi instrument dlya kompozitorov." Moskva (?), Soyuz Kompozitorov RSFSR, 1965.

925. "Music." In American Council of Learned Societies Newsletter. Special Supplement, Computerized Research in the Humanities: A Survey (June 1966), 38.

926. "Music of the future." American Record Guide, XXI (May 1955), 280.

927. "Music of the future?" Mademoiselle, L (Dec. 1959),

94.

928. "Music of the future." Time, LXVIII (July 2, 1956), 36.

929. "Music transcription by computer." Computing News, V, 17 (Sept. 1, 1957), 108.

930. "Música en la era atómica." Buenos Aires Musical, XVIII, 289 (1963), 6.

931. "Musik aus der Schreibmaschine (Hannover)." Melos, XXVI (May 1959), 154.

932. "Musik der Elektronenröhre." Die Musikwoche, XIV (1954), 195.

933. "Musique concrète." In The International Cyclopedia of Music and Musicians, 9th ed. New York, Dodd, Mead and Co., 1964, 1432.

934. "La musique concrète." La Vie musicale, I (Oct. 1951), 12.

935. Mycielski, Zygmunt. "Dwie strony medalu na temat VI 'Warszawskiej Jesieni.'" Ruch Muzyczny, VI, 21 (1962), 2.

936. Myers, Rollo H. "French music since the war." Dublin Review, CXXXI, 473 (1957), 84.

937. ------ "Music in France in the post-war decade." Proceedings of the Royal Musical Association, LXXXI (1954-1955), 93.

938. National Research Council of Canada, Technical Translations TT-601 to TT-612, TT-627, TT-646, TT-661, and TT-859. Ottawa, 1956, 1957. Translations by D.A. Sinclair of Technische Hausmitteilungen des Nordwestdeutschen Rundfunks, VI, 1-2 (1954); W. Kwasnik ("Klangästhetische ... "); J. Poullin ("L'apport ... "); A.A. Moles ("Essai de classification ... "); and A. Lietti ("Gli impianti ... ").

939. Nawrocki, Boleslaw. "Elektronika a Warsztat Kompozytorski." Ruch Muzyczny, IX, 24 (Jan. 1966), 5.

940. Nettel, Reginald. "Electric music by mathematics." _Music and Musicians_, VII, 1 (Sept. 29, 1958), 9.

941. ------ "Electronic music." _Monthly Musical Record_, LXXXVII (Sept.-Oct. 1957), 163.

942. "Das neue Buch: elektronische Musik in Italien." _Melos_, XXIV (May 1957), 139.

943. _Neue Musik in der Bundesrepublik Deutschland: Documentation 1957-_. Frankfurt, C.F. Peters, 1958-.

944. Neumann, P.G. and H. Schappert. "Komponieren mit elektronischen Rechenautomaten." _Nachrichtentechnische Zeitschrift_, XII, 8 (1959), 403. _Annales des Télécommunications_, 122446 (Dec. 1959).

945. "The new art of electronic music." _Electronics Illustrated_, II, 11 (Nov. 1959), 76.

946. "New Jersey: RCA electronic music synthesizer." _High Fidelity_, V (August 1955), 41.

947. "A new music synthesizer." _Tele-Tech_, XIV (March 1955), 80.

948. "'New thing' in longhair gets electronic roundup at N.Y. avant garde fete." _Variety_, CCXL (Sept. 8, 1965), 53.

949. "New York Philharmonic." _Musical America_, LXXXIV (Feb. 1964), 31.

950. Newmann, P. See Brooks, F.P., Jr.

951. "News and comments: Italy, electronic music." _Score_, 11 (March 1955), 67.

952. "No apology." _Time_, LXXVII (May 12, 1961), 51.

953. Nono, Luigi. "Die Entwicklung der Reihentechnik." _Darmstadter Beiträge zur neuen Musik_, I (1958).

954. ------ "Die neue Kompositionstechnik." _Gravesaner Blätter_, 6 (Dec. 1956), 19.

955. Nordwall, Ove. "Verför inte Electrofoni?" <u>Musikern</u>, 7-8 (July-August 1966), 12; 9 (Sept. 1966), 6.

956. Nørgaard, H. "Darmstadt-fragenter." <u>Dansk Musik-tidsskrift</u>, XXXVII, 6 (1962), 182.

957. ------ "Elektrofoni ... et middel til selvprøvelse." <u>Dansk Musiktidsskrift</u>, XXXIV (Sept. 1959), 149.

958. Nösselt, Volker. <u>Die Tonhöhenbewegungsinformation und ihre Perzeptionsverhaltensweisen in Geräuschen</u>. Utrecht, Rijksuniversiteit, Studio voor Elektronische Muziek, 1966 (mimeograph).

959. "Note on compositions developed from existing sound: traffic, brakes, etc." <u>Music and Musicians</u>, II (Feb. 1954), 22.

960. "NYC notes: Pierre Boulez, Otto Luening, Vladimir Ussachevsky -- 'Music in the Making' series at Cooper Union." <u>International Musician</u>, LI (March 1953), 13.

961. Oesch, Hans. "Einführung in die elektronische Musik." <u>Universitas</u>, XI (Feb. 1956), 167.

962. Olson, Harry F. "Electronic aid to composers." <u>Franklin Institute Journal</u>, CCLXX (July 1961), 78.

963. ------ <u>Musical engineering</u>. New York, McGraw-Hill, 1952.

964. ------ <u>Musical engineering</u>. Reviewed in <u>Audio Engineering</u>, XXXVI (August 1952), 9.

965. ------ "RCA electronic synthesizer a symbol of things to come." <u>Variety</u>, CC (Oct. 19, 1955), 46.

966. ------ and Herbert Belar. "Aid to music composition employing a random probability system." <u>Journal of the Acoustical Society of America</u>, XXXIII, 9 (Sept. 1961), 1163.

967. ------ and ------ "Electronic music synthesizer." <u>Journal of the Acoustical Society of America</u>,

XXVII, 5 (May 1955), 595.

968. —————— and —————— See Barbour, J. Murray.

969. ——————, ——————, and J. Timmens. "Electronic music
     synthesis: the Mark II R.C.A. Synthesizer." Jour-
     nal of the Acoustical Society of America, XXXII,
     3 (March 1960), 311.

970. "$175,000 Rockefeller fund gift for electronic
     music." Musical Courier, CLIX (Feb. 1959), 42.

971. Onnen, Frank. "Parijs: Pierre Schaeffer en de
     musique concrète." Mens en Melodie, XV (July
     1960), 218.

972. Oram, Daphne. "Electronic music, the present and
     the potential." Musical Events, XV (Dec. 1960),
     20.

973. —————— "How to make new music." The Tape Recorder,
     (June 1959).

974. —————— "Making musique concrète." Hi Fi News,
     (April 1958).

975. Otsuki, S. "An attempt at machine composition
     by machine experience." Information Processing
     in Japan, IV (1964).

976. Paap, Wouter. "Elektronische muziek." Mens en
     Melodie, XI (Sept. 1956), 265.

977. —————— "Muziek en soniek." Mens en Melodie, XVII
     (July 1962), 197.

978. Pade, Else Marie. "Lydprofetier?" Dansk Musik-
     tidsskrift, XXXII (May 1957), 38.

979. —————— "Tonens rumfart tur-retur; Eksperimental
     kongres, Verdensudstillingen, Bruxelles, 5.-10.
     oktober 1958." Nordisk Musikkultur, VII (Dec.
     1958), 104.

980. Paik, Nam June, et al. "Die Fluxus-Leute." Magnum
     (Köln), 47 (April 1963), 32.

981. Paisley, William J. "Twilight of the musicians." HiFi/Stereo Review, V (August 1960), 34.

982. ------ "Victim of the vacuum tube." Selmer Bandwagon, IX, 3 (Sept. 1961).

983. "Paris: several comments" (Kagel). Guide du concert, 259-260 (Feb. 12, 1960), 411.

984. "Park Lane group." The Strad, LXXIV (June 1963), 65.

985. Parker, M.E. "New horizons for the composer -- drawn sound." Musical America, LXXII (Nov. 15, 1952), 8.

986. Parmenter, Ross. "Electronic studio here aided by large grant." The New York Times, CVIII (Jan. 18, 1959), section 2, 9.

987. Patkowski, Jozef. "Skladatel v experimentalnom studiu." Slovenská Hudba, VIII, 4 (1964), 108.

988. ------ "Z zagadnien muzyki eksperymentalnej." Muzyka, IV, 3 (1959), 81.

989. Patmore, Derek. "Atomic age composer" (Stockhausen). Music and Musicians, XIII (Sept. 1965), 34.

990. Payne, Anthony. "Recitals: on the right track?" Music and Musicians, XI (July 1963), 10.

991. Pearsall, R. "Musique concrète and tradition." Musical Opinion, LXXXVI (June 1963), 531.

992. Pedersen, Paul. "The mel scale." Journal of Music Theory, IX, 2 (Winter 1965), 295.

993. Peignot, Jérome. "De la musique concrète à l'acousmatique." Esprit, XXVIII, 280 (Jan. 1960), 111.

994. Pensdorfova, E. "Predzvest nebo doznivani?" Hudební Rozhledy, XVII, 11 (1964), 454.

995. Pepper, Charles E. "The computer -- big machine on campus." University, A Princeton Quarterly, 29

(Summer 1966), 6.

996. "The perfect instrument." Woodwind World, III, 9 (1960), 15.

997. Perle, George. "Current chronicle: Germany." The Musical Quarterly, XLVI, 4 (Oct. 1960), 517.

998. Perspectives of New Music. Reviewed in Journal of Music Theory, VII, 2 (1963), 262.

999. Perspectives of New Music. Reviewed in Journal of the American Musicological Society, XVII, 1 (1964), 110.

1000. Perspectives of New Music. Reviewed in The Musical Quarterly, L, 1 (Jan. 1964), 107.

1001. Pestalozza, Luigi. "Musica applicata: impiego elettronico." Musica d'oggi, II (July 1959), 316.

1002. ------ "L'ultima avanguardia: post-Weberniani, concerti ed elettronici." Ricordiana (nuova serie), II (July 1956), 333.

1003. Peterson, R.H. "The design of electronic music instruments." Proceedings of the National Electronics Conference, XIV (1958), 212. Annales des Télécommunications, 123364 (Jan. 1960).

1004. "Petit lexique de musique expérimentale et électronique." Esprit, XXVIII, 280 (Jan. 1960), 121.

1005. Petri, Horst. "Identität von Sprache und Musik." Melos, XXXII, 10 (Oct. 1965), 345.

1006. Petrillo, James C. "Man, machine, music and musicians." International Musician, LIII (April 1955), 16.

1007. Petzoldt, H. "Studioanlagen für Stereophonie"/ "Stereo-equipment for studios." Gravesaner Blätter/Gravesano Review, IV, 15-16 (1960), 126/131.

1008. Peyser, Joan. "New music." Vogue, CXLVII (Feb. 1, 1966), 176.

78

1009. Pfeiffer, John F. "Living with the bugaboo." The New York Times, CXV (Sept. 25, 1966), M 3.

1010. Pfrogner, Hermann. "Elektronik -- Lust am Untergang?" Neue Zeitschrift für Musik, CXVIII (Sept. 1957), 484.

1011. Philippot, Michel. "Espace vital." La Revue musicale, 244 (1959), 32.

1012. ------ "Musique et acoustique." In La musique et ses problèmes contemporains 1953-1963. Paris, René Julliard (Cahiers de la compagnie Madeleine Renaud -- Jean-Louis Barrault, 41), 1963, 60.

1013. ------ "La musique et les machines." Situation de la recherche, Cahiers d'études de radio-télévision, 27-28 (Sept.-Dec. 1960), 274. Paris, Flammarion.

1014. "The Philips Pavilion at the 1958 Brussels World's Fair." Philips Technical Review, XX, 1-3 (1959).

1015. Phillips, A. "Osmond Kendall's marvellous music machine." MacLean's Magazine, (June 11, 1955), 22.

1016. Pickering, N.C. "Electronic simulation of organ sounds." Audio, XLVII (June 1963), 21.

1017. Pickler, Andrew G. "Musical transfer functions and processed music." Institute of Radio Engineers Transactions on Audio, AU-10, 2 (March-April 1962), 47.

1018. Pierce, John R. "The computer as a musical instrument." Journal of the Audio Engineering Society, VIII, 2 (April 1960), 139.

1019. ------ "Computers and music." New Scientist, XXV, 431 (Feb. 18, 1965), 423.

1020. ------ Electrons, waves, and messages. Garden City, Hanover House, 1956.

1021. ------ Letter. Scientific American, CXCIV, 4 (1956), 18.

1022. ------ "Portrait of the machine as a young artist."
Playboy, XII, 6 (June, 1965), 124.

1023. ------ Symbols, signals and noise. New York, Harper, 1961.

1024. ------ See Mathews, Max V.

1025. ------, Max V. Mathews and J.C. Risset. "Weitere
Experimente im musikalischen Gebrauch des Elektro-
nenrechners"/"Further experiments on the use of
the computer in connection with music." Gravesaner Blätter/Gravesano Review, 27-28 (Nov. 1965),
85/92.

1026. Pierret, Marc. "Notre aimable clientèle (témoi-
gnages)." La Revue musicale, 247 (June 1959),
9.

1027. Pike, W.S. and C.N. Hoyler. "Synthesizing timbres
for electronic musical tones." Electronics, XXXII
(May 29, 1959), 42. Annales des Télécommunications,
119132 (August-Sept. 1959).

1028. Pinkerton, Richard C. "Information theory and
melody." Scientific American, CXCIV, 2 (Feb.
1956), 77.

1029. Piper, David. "Electronic courses." Composer,
21 (Autumn 1966), 33.

1030. Pisk, Paul A. See Ulrich, Homer.

1031. Plaetner, J. "De første famlende skridt." Dansk
Musiktidsskrift, XXXV, 5 (May 1960), 161.

1032. "Plans for new electronic music laboratory at Columbia University." Journal of the Acoustical
Society of America, XXXI (1959), 1388.

1033. "Plop: a demonstration of the Side Man." The New
Yorker, XXXVI (April 23, 1960), 35.

1034. Pociej, B. "Koncert Muzyki electronowej i konkret-
ney (Warsaw)." Ruch Muzyczny, VII, 22 (1963), 17.

1035. Polaczek, W. "Die elektronische AWB Orgel." Radio-Technik, XI (1954), 409.

1036. Porena, Boris. "L'avanguardia musicale di Darmstadt." La Rassegna musicale, XXVIII, 3 (March 1958), 208.

1037. Porter, Andrew. "Some new British composers." In Lang and Broder, eds., Contemporary music in Europe. New York, G. Schirmer, 1965, 12. The Musical Quarterly, LI, 1 (Jan. 1965), 12.

1038. Pospishil, V. "Krizis tvorcheskoy fantazii?" Sovetskaya Muzyka, XXVI (Feb. 1962), 124.

1039. Potter, R.K. "New scientific tools for the arts." Journal of Aesthetics and Art Criticism, X, 2 (Dec. 1951), 126.

1040. Poullin, Jacques. "The application of recording techniques to the production of new musical materials and forms. Applications to 'musique concrète.'" Ottawa, National Research Council of Canada, Technical Translation TT-646, 1957 (translation of 1041).

1041. ------ "L'apport des techniques d'entregistrement dans la fabrication de matières et de formes musicales nouvelles. Applications à la musique concrète." L'Onde électrique, XXXIV, 324 (1954), 282.

1042. ------ "Les chaînes électro-acoustiques." Situation de la recherche, Cahiers d'études de radio-télévision, 27-28 (Sept.-Dec. 1960), 229. Paris, Flammarion.

1043. ------ "Musique concrète." In Winckel, ed., Klang-struktur der Musik. Berlin, Verlag für Radio-Foto-Kinotechnik, 1955, 109.

1044. ------ "L'oreille et le malentendu." La Revue musicale, 244 (1959), 37.

1045. ------ "Son et espace." La Revue musicale, 236 (1957), 105.

1046. Pousseur, Henri. "A propos d'électronique musicale -- la musique concrète." Cahiers français
(?), (Jan. 1955).

1047. ------ "Domaines à venir." In La musique et ses
problèmes contemporains 1953-1963. Paris, René
Julliard (Cahiers de la Compagnie Madeleine Renaud -- Jean-Louis Barrault, 41), 1963, 86.

1048. ------ "Musik, Form und Praxis"/"Music, form and
practice." Die Reihe, VI/6 (1960/1964), 71/77
(Reply to Ruwet, "Von den Widersprüchen der seriellen Sprache").

1049. ------ "Musique électronique, musique sérielle."
Cahiers musicaux, 12 (March 1957), 50.

1050. ------ "La nuova sensibilità musicale." Incontri
musicale, 2 (May 1958).

1051. ------ "Scambi." Gravesaner Blätter/Gravesano Review, IV, 13 (1959), 36/48.

1052. ------ "Strukturen des neuen Baustoffs"/"Formal elements in a new compositional material." Die Reihe,
I/1 (1955/1958), 42/30.

1053. ------ "Textes sur l'expression." In La musique
et ses problèmes contemporains 1953-1963. Paris,
René Julliard (Cahiers de la Compagnie Madeleine
Renaud -- Jean-Louis Barrault, 41), 1963, 169.

1054. ------ "Theorie und Praxis in der neuesten Musik."
Darmstadter Beiträge zur neuen Musik, II (1959).

1055. ------ "Zur Methodik"/"Outline of a method." Die
Reihe, III/3 (1957/1959), 46/44.

1056. Powell, Mel. "Electronic music and musical newness."
The American Scholar, XXXV, 2 (Spring, 1966),
290.

1057. ------ "Volley for Varèse." Saturday Review, XLIII
(Dec. 31, 1960), 34.

1058. Prieberg, Fred K. "Elektronische Musik aus Lochstreifen." <u>Melos</u>, XXXI (April 1964), 118.

1059. ------ "Die Emanzipation des Geraüsches." <u>Melos</u>, XXIV (Jan. 1957), 9.

1060. ------ "Erste elektronische Partitur." <u>Neue Zeit-schrift für Musik</u>, CXVIII (April 1957), 241.

1061. ------ "Experimentell musik i Sovjet." <u>Nutida Musik</u>, VII, 1 (1963-64). In German: <u>Magnum</u>, (April 1963).

1062. ------ "Honeggers elektronisches Experiment." <u>Me-los</u>, XXIII (Jan. 1956), 20.

1063. ------ "Italiens elektronische Musik." <u>Melos</u>, XXV (June 1958), 194.

1064. ------ <u>Knaurs Lexikon</u>. Stuttgart, Droemer, 1961.

1065. ------ <u>Lexikon der neuen Musik</u>. Freiburg/München, Karl Alber, 1958.

1066. ------ <u>Lexikon der neuen Musik</u>. Reviewed in <u>Melos</u>, XXVI (April 1959), 112.

1067. ------ <u>Lexikon der neuen Musik</u>. Reviewed in <u>Musical America</u>, LXXIX (Jan. 15, 1959), 19.

1068. ------ <u>Lexikon der neuen Musik</u>. Reviewed in <u>Neue Zeitschrift für Musik</u>, CXX (May 1959), 288.

1069. ------ <u>Lexikon der neuen Musik</u>. Reviewed in <u>Oester-reichische Musikzeitschrift</u>, XIV (Jan. 1959), 40.

1070. ------ <u>Musica ex Machina: über das Verhältnis von Musik und Technik</u>. Berlin, Verlag Ullstein, 1960.

1071. ------ <u>Musica ex Machina</u>. Reviewed by Otto C. Luening in <u>Julliard Review</u>, VII, 3 (Fall 1960), 23.

1072. ------ <u>Musica ex Machina</u>. Reviewed in <u>Journal of Aesthetics and Art Criticism</u>, XXI, 1 (1962), 10.

1073. ------ <u>Musica ex Machina</u>. Reviewed in <u>Melos</u>, XXXI (July-August 1964), 230.

1074. ------ Musica ex Machina. Reviewed in Music and
        Letters, XLI (July 1960), 279.

1075. ------ Musica ex Machina. Reviewed in The Music
        Review, XXII, 1 (1961), 63.

1076. ------ "Musik der Zukunft." Oesterreichische Musik-
        zeitschrift, XI (Nov. 1954), 351.

1077. ------ "'Musik der Zukunft' -- und ihr Wesen."
        Schweizerische Musikzeitung, XCV (Sept. 1955),
        337.

1078. ------ Musik des technischen Zeitalters. Zürich,
        Atlantis Verlag, 1956.

1079. ------ Musik des technischen Zeitalters. Reviewed
        in Melos, XXIV (June 1957), 177.

1080. ------ Musik des technischen Zeitalters. Reviewed
        in Musica, XI (March 1957), 181.

1081. ------ Musik des technischen Zeitalters. Reviewed
        in Neue Zeitschrift für Musik, CXVIII (Nov. 1967),
        647.

1082. ------ "Musik: Töne aus der Elektronröhre." Monat,
        X (Nov. 1957), 62.

1083. ------ "Musik und Elektroakustik: Internationaler
        Kongress in Gravesano." Das Musikleben, VII (Oct.
        1954), 361.

1084. ------ "Schrotthaufen der Esoterik? Kongress für
        elektronische und konkrete Musik." Zeitschrift
        für Musik, CXVI (August-Sept. 1955), 509.

1085. ------ "Tagung für elektronische und konkrete
        Musik." Das Musikleben, VIII (July-August 1955),
        283.

1086. "Les principes de composition de la musique algo-
        rithmique par des ensembles à traiter l'informa-
        tion." Electro-calcul, IV, 2 (March-April 1962),
        19.

1087. "The progress of science: electronic music." Discovery, XIX (Jan. 1958), 4.

1088. "Quarter-ear music." World of Music, 3 (Jan. 1958), 11.

1089. Quastler, H. "Discussion." In Cherry, ed., Information theory -- third London symposium. New York, Academic Press, 1956, 168.

1090. Rabb, Bernard P. "Electronic music is valid!" Music Journal, XIX, 7 (Oct. 1961), 60.

1091. Rakowski, A. "Metody realizacji muzyki konkretnej." Muzyka, III, 3 (1958), 58.

1092. ------ "Muzyka Konkretna we Francji w letach 1949-55." Muzyka, III, 1-2 (1958), 134.

1093. ------ "O zastosowaniu cyfrowych maszyn matematycznych do muzyki." Muzyka, VII, 3 (1962), 83.

1094. Randall, J.K. "A report from Princeton (forum: computer research)." Perspectives of New Music, III, 2 (Spring-Summer 1965), 84.

1095. Randolph, David. "Machine-made music." Music Journal, XVII, 3 (March 1959), 22.

1096. ------ "A new music made with a machine." Horizon, I, 3 (Jan. 1959), 50.

1097. Rapoport, Anatole. "What is information?" Etc., X, (Summer 1953), 247.

1098. Raug, Hans. "Laufzeitstereophonie"/"Time delay stereophony." Gravesaner Blätter/Gravesano Review, IV, 13 (1959), 71/77.

1099. Rawsthorne, Alan. "Electronic courses." Composer, 21 (Autumn 1966), 33.

1100. "RCA electronic device can produce piano tone." Music Trade Review, CXIV (Feb. 1955), 26.

1101. Regener, Eric. "A linear music transcription for

computer input." Princeton, N.J., Princeton University Department of Music, March 23, 1964.

1102. Reich, Herbert. See Douglas, Alan L.M.

1103. Reich, Willi. "Das elektroakustische Experimentalstudio Gravesano." Schweizerische Musikzeitung, XCIX (Sept. 1959), 321.

1104. ------ "Gravesano an den Grenzen der Musik." Melos, XXVIII (Nov. 1961), 372.

1105. Die Reihe: Information über serielle Musik. Reviewed in Journal of Music Theory, III (April 1959), 155.

1106. Die Reihe. Reviewed in Melos, XXII (Dec. 1955), 352.

1107. Die Reihe. Reviewed in The Musical Times, C (Jan. 1959), 19.

1108. Die Reihe. Reviewed in Score, 13 (Sept. 1955), 23.

1109. Reiner, A. "Technik provoziert Kunst." Melos, XXVII (Sept. 1960), 275.

1110. Reisfeld, B. "Symphonie der Vögel Nr. 2." Musica, X (Dec. 1956), 852.

1111. Répertoire international des musiques expérimentales. Paris, Service de la Recherche de la Radiodiffusion-Télévision Française, 1962.

1112. Reti, Jean. "An international conference of composers." Tempo, 55-56 (Autumn-Winter 1960), 6.

1113. Rich, Alan. "Columbia offers electronic concert." Musical America, LXXXI (June 1961), 68.

1114. Richard, Albert. "Quatre ans après." La Revue musicale, 236 (1957), 1.

1115. Richardson, E.G. "Electro-acoustics applied to musical instruments." Acustica, IV, 1 (1954), 212.

1116. ------ "Electrophonic instruments." In Grove's
      Dictionary of Music and Musicians, 5th ed., II.
      London and New York, Macmillan, 1954, 905.

1117. ------ "The production and analysis of tone by
      electrical means." Proceedings of the Royal Musi-
      cal Association, LXVI (1939-1940), 53.

1118. Righini, P. See Caciotti, M.

1119. Ringer, Alexander L. "Musical composition in mo-
      dern Israel." In Lang and Broder, eds., Contem-
      porary music in Europe. New York, G. Schirmer,
      1965, 282. The Musical Quarterly, LI, 1 (Jan.
      1965), 282.

1120. Risset, J.C. See Pierce, John R.

1121. Roberts, Arthur. "An all-FORTRAN music-generating
      computer program." Journal of the Audio Engineer-
      ing Society, XIV, 1 (Jan. 1966), 17.

1122. ------ "Some notes on computer-generated music"
      (abstract). Journal of the Acoustical Society
      of America, XXXIX, 6 (June 1966), 1245.

1123. Robin, H. "U.S. experiments." The New York Times,
      CV (July 22, 1956), section 2, 7.

1124. Robin, Jon. "Darmstadt report: note on musique
      concrète and electronic music." Musical Courier,
      CXLVIII (Oct. 15, 1953), 16.

1125. Robison, Judith. "Laboratory for sounds." Music
      Magazine, CLXIV (May 1962), 18.

1126. Rochberg, George. "Current chronicle: Canada."
      The Musical Quarterly, XLVII, 1 (Jan. 1961), 103.

1127. ------ "The new image of music." Perspectives of
      New Music, II, 1 (Fall-Winter 1963), 67.

1128. Rognoni, Luigi. "La musica 'elettronica' e il
      problema della technica." Aut Aut, 36 (Nov.
      1956), 450.

1129. Rohwer, Jens. Neueste Musik: ein kritischer Bericht. Stuttgart, Ernst Klett Verlag, 1964, 75.

1130. Rondi, Brunello. Il Cammino della musica d'oggi e l'esparienza elettronica. Padova, Rebellato, 1959.

1131. ------ Il Cammino della musica d'oggi e l'esperienza elettronica. Reviewed in La Rassegna musicale. XXX, 1 (1960), 97.

1132. Rorem, Ned. "Is new music new?" American Record Guide, XXXII (May 1966), 776.

1133. Rosenberg, Victor. "Disques." Esprit, XXVIII, 280 (Jan. 1960), 133.

1134. Rostand, Claude. "Tendenzen der französischen Musik." Melos, XVIII (June-July 1951), 175.

1135. Roth, H. "USA: avantgardistische Musik." Musik und Gesellschaft, XIV (June 1964), 380.

1136. "Rozmowa z Josefem Patkowskim o Studiu Eksperymentalnym." Ruch Muzyczny, VII, 1 (1963), 3.

1137. Rübenach, Bernhard. "Musique concrète." Blätter und Bilder, 2 (May-June 1959), 47.

1138. Ruppel, K.H. "Initiatives allemandes analogues au Domaine musical." In La musique et ses problèmes contemporains 1953-1963. Paris, René Julliard (Cahiers de la compagnie Madeleine Renaud -- Jean-Louis Barrault, 41), 1963, 279.

1139. Rupprath, R. See Meyer-Eppler, Werner.

1140. Russolo, Luigi. L'Art des bruits. Paris, Éditions Richard-Masse, 1954.

1141. Rust, H.H. "Elektrische Klangsynthese." Die Umschau in Wissenschaft und Technik, LIV (1954), 356.

1142. Ruwet, Nicolas. "Von den Widersprüchen der seriellen Sprache"/"Contradictions within the serial

language." <u>Die Reihe</u>, VI/6 (1960/1964), 59/65.
"Contradictions du langage sérial." <u>Revue Belge
de Musicologie</u>, XIII, 1-4 (1959), 83.

1143. Saathen, Friedrich. "Musik und Technik." <u>Neue
Zeitschrift für Musik</u>, CXXIII (Sept. 1962), 396.

1144. Sabiston, C. "Engineers lead composers." <u>Musical
America</u>, LXXX (Oct. 1960), 33.

1145. Sala, Oskar. "Experimentelle und theoretische
Grundlagen des Trautoniums." <u>Frequenz</u>, II (Dec.
1948), 315; III (Jan. 1949), 13.

1146. ------ "Das Mixtur-Trautonium." <u>Melos</u>, XVII (Sept.
1950). <u>Physikalische Blätter</u>, VI, 9 (1950).

1147. ------ "Mixtur-Trautonium und Studio-Technik"/"Mix-
ture-Trautonium and studio technique." <u>Gravesa-
ner Blätter/Gravesano Review</u> VI, 23-24 (1962), 42/
53.

1148. ------ "Das neue Mixtur-Trautonium." <u>Das Musik-
leben</u>, VI (1953), 346.

1149. ------ "Subharmonische elektrische Klangsynthesen."
In Winckel, ed., <u>Klangstruktur der Musik</u>. Berlin,
Verlag für Radio-Foto-Kinotechnik, 1955, 89.

1150. Salimbeni, A. "Taccuino musicale Americano." <u>Mu-
sica d'oggi</u>, III (Dec. 1960), 446.

1151. "Le salon a fermé ses portes." <u>Musique et Radio</u>,
LII (March 1962), 91.

1152. Salzman, Eric. "Davidovsky: <u>Three synchronisms</u>"
(review of recording). <u>High Fidelity</u>, XVI, 9
(Sept. 1966), 94.

1153. ------ "From composer to magnetron to you." <u>High
Fidelity</u>, X, 8 (August 1960), 40.

1154. ------ "Montages of sound." <u>The New York Times</u>,
CVIII (March 15, 1959), section 10, 3.

1155. ------ "Music from the electronic universe." <u>High</u>

Fidelity, XIV, 8 (August 1964), 54.

1156. ------ "New musical conceptions realized by electronic means" (review of recordings). High Fidelity, XIII, 8 (August 1963), 91.

1157. ------ "New York report: the new virtuosity." Perspectives of New Music, I, 2 (Spring 1963), 174.

1158. ------ "Records: Vortex." The New York Times, CVIII (June 21, 1959), section 2, 10.

1159. Sargeant, Winthrop. "Musical events" (demonstration of Ussachevsky's music). The New Yorker, XLII (May 28, 1966), 86.

1160. ------ "Musical events" (Gassman's Electronics). The New Yorker, XXXVII (April 1, 1961), 126.

1161. Savelli, Vittorio. See Caciotti, M.

1162. Sayre, K.M. and F.J. Crosson, eds. The modeling of mind -- computers and intelligence. Notre Dame, Indiana, University of Notre Dame Press, 1963.

1163. Sborník přednášek o problémech elektronické hudby (2 volumes). Praha (?), Dilia, 1964.

1164. Scerri, A. and Karlhans Weisse. "Das Experimentalstudio Gravesano." Gravesaner Blätter, 1 (July 1955), 5.

1165. Schaeffer, Myron S. "The creation of melodic contours from non-melodic raw material without loss of text or timbre." Journal of the Audio Engineering Society, XI, 1 (Jan. 1963), 55.

1166. ------ "The electronic music studio of the University of Toronto." Journal of Music Theory, VIII, 1 (Spring 1963), 73.

1167. ------ "An extension of tone-row techniques through electronic pitch control." Journal of the International Folk Music Council, XVI (1964), 95.

1168. ------ "The Hamograph, a new amplitude-rhythm con-
trol device for the production of electronic music."
Institute of Radio Engineers Transactions on Audio,
AU-10, 1 (Jan.-Feb. 1962), 22.

1169. ------ "A simple method for control of multi-signal
recording." Audio Engineering Society Preprint
No. 299, 1963.

1170. ------ "The space age and electronic music." Per-
forming Arts in Canada, II, 1 (Winter 1963), 5.

1171. ------ "Synthesis and manipulation of natural sounds
in electronic music for films." Journal of the
Society of Motion Picture and Television Engineers,
LXXIII (Feb. 1964), 128.

1172. Schaeffer, Pierre. À la recherche d'une musique
concrète. Paris, Éditions du Seuil, 1952.

1173. ------ À la recherche d'une musique concrète. Reviewed in Monthly Musical Record, LXXXII (Sept.
1952), 169.

1174. ------ À la recherche d'une musique concrète. Reviewed in Musica, VII (July-August 1953), 359.

1175. ------ À la recherche d'une musique concrète. Reviewed in Musical America, LXXIII (Jan. 1953), 25.

1176. ------ À la recherche d'une musique concrète. Reviewed in La Rassegna musicale, XXII (Oct. 1952),
36.

1177. ------ "Anamorphose entre musique et acoustique."
Cahiers d'études de radio-télévision, 19, (1958),
227.

1178. ------ "Anmerkung zu den 'zeitbedingten Wechsel-
wirkungen'"/"Note on time relationships." Gravesaner Blätter/Gravesano Review, V, 17 (1960), 12/
50.

1179. ------ "Ce qui est en question." Situation de la
recherche, Cahiers d'études de radio-télévision,
27-28 (Sept.-Dec. 1960), 3. Paris, Flammarion.

1180. ------ "Concrète (musique)." In _Encyclopédie de la musique_. Paris, Fasquelle, 1958, 576.

1181. ------ "Le contrepoint du son et de l'image." _Cahiers du cinéma_, XVIII, 108 (June 1960), 7.

1182. ------ "De l'expérimentation en musique." _Situation de la recherche, Cahiers d'études de radio-télévision_, 27-28 (Sept.-Dec. 1960), 251. Paris, Flammarion.

1183. ------ "Le groupe de recherches musicales de La Radiodiffusion-Télévision Française." _La Revue musicale_, 244 (1959), 49.

1184. ------ "Introduction à la musique concrète." _Polyphonie_, 6 (1950), 30.

1185. ------ "L'intrusion de l'électroacoustique en musique." _Gravesaner Blätter_, 2-3 (Jan. 1956), 38.

1186. ------ "Lettre à Albert Richard." _La Revue musicale_, 236 (1957), iii.

1187. ------ "La main passe." _La Revue musicale_, 247 (June 1959), 4.

1188. ------ "Das Missverständnis von Donaueschingen." _Melos_, XXI (May 1953), 138.

1189. ------ "La musique concrète." _La Vie musicale_, I (July-August 1951), 8.

1190. ------ "Musique concrète et connaissance de l'objet musical." _Revue Belge de Musicologie_, XIII, 1-4 (1959), 62.

1191. ------ "Musique expérimentale." _Musical Information Record_ (Paris), 13-14 (Summer-Autumn 1954), 24.

1192. ------ "L'objet musical." _La Revue musicale_, 212 (1952), 65.

1193. ------ "Phonogene à clavier: notion d'un coup de tam-tam." _Guide du concert_, 237 (June 5, 1959),

1194. ------ "La recherche fondamentale en matière de radio et télévision." In Le Service de la recherche. Paris, La Radiodiffusion-Télévision Française, undated (c. 1961).

1195. ------ "Retour aux sources." Situation de la recherche, Cahiers d'études de radio-télévision, 27-28 (Sept.-Dec. 1960), 24. Paris, Flammarion.

1196. ------ "Le Service de la recherche." In Le Service de la recherche. Paris, La Radiodiffusion-Télévision Française, undated (c. 1961).

1197. ------ "Situation actuelle de la musique expérimentale." La Revue musicale, 244 (1959), 10.

1198. ------ Traité des objets musicaux. Paris, Éditions du Seuil, 1966.

1199. ------ "Vers une musique expérimentale." La Revue musicale, 236 (1957), 11.

1200. ------ "Vers une musique expérimentale." Reviewed in Guide du concert, 258 (Nov. 8, 1957), 258.

1201. ------ "Wechselwirkung zwischen Musik und Akustik"/ "The interplay between music and acoustics." Gravesaner Blätter/Gravesano Review, IV, 14 (1959), 51/61.

1202. Schappert, H. See Neumann, P.G.

1203. Schatz, Hilmar. "Stockhausens neue Tendenzen." Melos, XXV (Feb. 1958), 67.

1204. Scherchen, Hermann. "Dépassement de l'orchestre." La Revue musicale, 236 (1957), 56.

1205. ------ "The musical past and the electronic future." Saturday Review, XLVII (Oct. 31, 1964), 63 (translated by M. Bernheimer).

1206. ------ "Stockhausen und die Zeit"/"Stockhausen and time." Gravesaner Blätter/Gravesano Review, IV,

13 (1959), 29/32.

1207. Schillinger, Joseph. "Electricity, a musical libe-
rator." Modern Music, VIII, 3 (March 1931), 26.

1208. ------ "Electronic instruments." Book XII, Chapter
5 in The Schillinger system of musical composition,
volume II. New York, Carl Fischer, 1941, 1544.

1209. Schloezer, Boris de. "Musique concrète, musique
abstraite, musique." La Nouvelle revue française
I (May 1953).

1210. ------ "Musique contemporaine et musique moderne."
La Nouvelle revue française, II (March 1954).

1211. ------ "Retour à Descartes." La Nouvelle revue
française, I (June 1953).

1212. Schmidt-Garre, H. "Elektronischer Schock in München." Melos, XXIV (Feb. 1957), 50.

1213. Schnebel, Dieter. "Karlheinz Stockhausen." Die
Reihe, IV/4 (1958/1960), 119/122.

1214. ------ "Nachwort: Einführung des Herausgebers."
In K. Stockhausen, Texte, Band 2. Köln, Verlag
M. DuMont Schauberg, 1964, 264.

1215. Schönberg, Arnold. Harmonielehre. Wien, Universal
Edition, 1911.

1216. Schonberg, Harold C. "The avant-garde, very busy,
is scorned by the establishment." National Music
Council Bulletin, XXV, 1 (1964), 18.

1217. ------ "The future of the symphony." The New York
Times, CXIV (Oct. 24, 1965), X19.

1218. ------ "Holland festival." The New York Times,
CX (July 16, 1961), section 2, 7.

1219. ------ "Maverick, revolutionary, and father to a
generation" (Varèse: obituary). The New York Times,
CXIV (Nov. 14, 1965), section 2, 11.

1220. ------ "Music from electronics." <u>The New York Times</u>, CVI (Jan. 27, 1957), section 2, 15.

1221. ------ "Nothing but us speakers." <u>The New York Times</u>, CX (May 21, 1961), section 2, 9.

1222. ------ "Phantom of the opera." <u>The New York Times</u>, CXV (Feb. 6, 1966), magazine section, 11.

1223. ------ "Sounds on tape." <u>The New York Times</u>, CXII (May 12, 1963), section 2, 9.

1224. ------ "Splitting the octave." <u>The New York Times</u>, CV (June 17, 1956), section 2, 9.

1225. ------ "Too much hoopla (Philharmonic's avant-garde series)." <u>The New York Times</u>, CXIII (Feb. 2, 1964), section 2, 11.

1226. Schortt, John Ramsen. "Aurelio de la Vega, un compositor de las Américas." <u>Revista Musical Chilena</u>, XVII, 84 (April–June 1963), 62.

1227. Schreiber, E. "Die elektonische 'Minshall Orgel.'" <u>Radio Fernsehen</u>, III (Nov. 1954), 325. <u>Annales des Télécommunications</u>, X, 71406 (Feb. 1955).

1228. ------ "Ein neuartiger elektronischer Klang- und Geräuscherzeuger." <u>OIRT Zeitschrift, Rundfunk und Fernsehen</u>, 2 (1964).

1229. Schroeder, M.R. and B.F. Logan. "'Colorless' artificial reverberation." <u>Institute of Radio Engineers Transactions on Audio</u>, AU-9, 6 (Nov.-Dec. 1961), 209.

1230. Schubert, Kurt, ed. <u>Theorie und Praxis der Hörgeräteanpassung, sowie Probleme der Begutachtung.</u> Stuttgart, Georg Thieme Verlag, 1960.

1231. Schuh, Willi. "'Musique concrète' und elektronische Musik." In <u>Von neuen Musik</u>. Zürich, Atlantis Verlag, 1955, 222.

1232. Schuller, Gunther. "Conversation with Varèse." <u>Perspectives of New Music</u>, III, 2 (Spring-Summer

1965), 32.

1233. ------ "The new German music for radio." <u>The Satur-</u>
<u>day Review</u>, XLV (Jan. 13, 1962), 62.

1234. Schütz, Heinz. See Enkel, Fritz.

1235. Schwartz, Elliott. "Current chronicle: Brunswick,
Maine." <u>The Musical Quarterly</u>, LI, 4 (Oct. 1965),
680.

1236. Scriabine, Marina. "Pierre Boulez et la musique
concrète." <u>La Revue musicale</u>, 215 (1952), 14.

1237. Searle, Humphrey. "Concrete music." In <u>Grove's</u>
<u>Dictionary of Music and Musicians</u>, 5th ed., IX,
appendix II. London and New York, Macmillan,
1954, 573. Supplementary volume, 1961, 80.

1238. ------ "Electrophonic music." In <u>Grove's Dictionary</u>
<u>of Music and Musicians</u>, 5th ed., IX, appendix II.
London and New York, Macmillan, 1954, 573. Supplementary volume, 1961, 120.

1239. Seawright, James. "What is electronic music?"
<u>Radio Electronics</u>, XXXVI (June, 1965), 36.

1240. Seay, Albert. "The composer of music and the computer." <u>Computers and Automation</u>, XIII, 8 (August
1964), 16.

1241. ------ "What is electronic music?" <u>Music Journal</u>,
XXI (March 1963), 26.

1242. "See longhair composers going electronic as way to
counter symph brushes." <u>Variety</u>, CCXIX (June 22,
1960), 45.

1243. Seeliger, Ronald. "Laboratorium der Klänge."
<u>Phonoprisma</u>, VI, 3 (1963), 54.

1244. Selden-Goth, Gisella. "The international music
scene: Italy -- publishing house set up for new
types of music by Aldo Bruzzichelli." <u>Musical</u>
<u>Courier</u>, CLXII, 1 (July 1960), 30.

1245. Semini, G.F. "Il laboratorio elettroacustico di Hermann Scherchen a Gravesano." La Scala, 139 (June 1961), 18.

1246. Sendhoff, H. See Meyer-Eppler, Werner.

1247. Sept ans de musique concrète: 1948-1955 (Group de Recherches de Musique Concrète de la Radiodif-fusion-Télévision Française). Paris, Centre d'Études Radiophoniques, 1955.

1248. Le Service de la recherche. Paris, La Radiodiffu-sion-Télévision Française, undated (c. 1961).

1249. Sessions, Roger. "Problems and issues facing the composer today." The Musical Quarterly, XLVI, 2 (April 1960), 159. In Lang, ed., Problems of modern music. New York, W.W. Norton, 1962, 21.

1250. "Seven sessions: criticism." The Music Review, XXII (August 1961), 229.

1251. Shannon, C.E. and Warren Weaver. The mathematical theory of communication. Urbana, University of Illinois Press, 1949.

1252. Shaw, Jane A. "Computers and the humanities." Electronic Age, XXIV, 4 (Spring 1965), 26.

1253. Shiotani, Hiroshi. See Takatsuji, Tsukasa.

1254. Shneerson, G. "Opera i elektronika." Sovetskaya Muzyka, XXIII (August 1959), 181.

1255. Shostakovich, Dmitri. "Art must reflect reality!" Music Journal, XX (Sept. 1962), 20.

1256. "Sick machine: Vortex." Time, LXXIII (Feb. 2, 1959), 45.

1257. Sieder, A.L. "Die überflüssige Windmaschine." Zeitschrift für Musik, CXVI (August-Sept. 1955), 456.

1258. Sigmon, Carl P. "Bethany Beardslee." Musical America, LXXXIV, 3 (March 1964), 42.

1259. ------ "Chamber music in New York." <u>Musical America</u>
LXXXIII (Feb. 1963), 33.

1260. ------ "Festival of the avant-garde." <u>Musical
America</u>, LXXXIV, (Oct. 1964), 52.

1261. ------ "Music in our time." <u>Musical America</u>, LXXX
LXXXIV, 5 (May 1964), 48.

1262. Silva, C. "Música experimental y música contem-
poranea." <u>Clave</u>, LI (May-June 1963), 22.

1263. Sinclair, D.A. See National Research Council of
Canada.

1264. Singer, Samuel L. "The national scene: Philadelphia" (Stockhausen's address to Art Alliance).
<u>Musical Courier</u>, CLIX (Feb. 1952), 32.

1265. "S' Julien le Pauvre." <u>Guide du concert</u>, 393 (June
22, 1963), 11.

1266. Skudrzyk, E. See Meyer-Eppler, Werner, ed.

1267. Slawson, A.W. "MUSE, a sound synthesizer." <u>Pro-
ceedings of the IFIPS Congress, Munich, 1962</u>.
Amsterdam, North Holland Publishing Company, 1962,
209.

1268. Slonimsky, Nicolas. "New music in Greece." In
Lang and Broder, eds., <u>Contemporary music in
Europe</u>. New York, G. Schirmer, 1965, 225. <u>The
Musical Quarterly</u>, LI, 1 (Jan. 1965), 225.

1269. Small, Arnold M. See Winckel, Fritz W.

1270. Smith, N. "Musica nova in USA." <u>Musikhandel</u>,
XII, 8 (1961), 418.

1271. Smith Brindle, Reginald. "The lunatic fringe.
I. Concrete music. II. Electronic music. III.
Computational composition." <u>The Musical Times</u>,
XCVII (1956), 246, 300, 354.

1272. ------ "Reports from abroad (Italy): The R.A.I.
Studio di fonologia musicale at Milan." <u>The</u>

Musical Times, XCIX, 1380 (Feb. 1958), 98.

1273. Snaith, William. *The irresponsible arts.* New York, Atheneum, 1964.

1274. Sonner, Rudolf. "Elektronische Musik, ihre drei Arbeitsberichte." *Zeitschrift für Musik*, CXVI (August-Sept. 1955), 449.

1275. ------ "Die Entwicklung der elektronischen Musik und ihre Instrumente." *Das Musikinstrument*, IV (1955), 216.

1276. ------ "Die Hohner-Multimonica II." *Instrumentenbau Zeitschrift*, VIII (1954), 170.

1277. "Sound of cybernetics: aleatoric music performed by the New York Philharmonic Orchestra." *Newsweek*, LXIII (Feb. 17, 1964), 88.

1278. "Sound of hell: score for film version of *No Exit.*" *Newsweek*, LX (Dec. 10, 1962), 86.

1279. "Sound stuff: tapesichord." *Newsweek*, XLIII (Jan. 11, 1954), 76.

1280. Sowa, John R. "A machine to compose music." In *Geniac Manual*. New York, Oliver Garfield, 1964.

1281. Spaeth, Sigmund. "In and out of tune (mechanization and robotism in music)." *Music Journal*, XX (Oct. 1962), 80.

1282. Spelman, F. "Germany's knights of the sound table." *Music Magazine*, CLXIV (July 1962), 10.

1283. Springer, Anton M. "Akustischer Tempo- und Tonlagenregler"/"Acoustic speed and pitch regulator." *Gravesaner Blätter/Gravesano Review*, IV, 13 (1959), 80/81

1284. ------ "Ein akustischer Zeitregler." *Gravesaner Blätter*, 1 (July 1955), 32.

1285. ------ "Rotierende Mehrfachköpfe"/"Rotating multiple magnetic heads." *Gravesaner Blätter/Gravesano*

Review, VI, 21 (1961), 38/48.

1286. ------ "Tonlagenregler und Informations-wandler"/
"A pitch regulator and information changer."
Gravesaner Blätter/Gravesano Review, III, 11-12
(1958), 3/7.

1287. ------ "Zwei Anwendungsbeispiele des Information-
wandlers"/"Two applications of the information
changer." Gravesaner Blätter/Gravesano Review,
VI, 23-24 (1962), 98/96.

1288. Stadlen, Peter. "Electronic music." The Musical
Times, CI, 1414 (Dec. 1960), 758.

1289. ------ "Musical survey." Musical Events, XV (May
1960), vii.

1290. Stam, Henk. "Het contactorgaan voor elektronische
muziek." Mens en Melodie, XIV (Feb. 1959), 45.

1291. ------ "'Orest' von Henk Badings." Das Musikleben,
VIII (June 1955), 217.

1292. Stanislav, Josef. "Unaveni hudbou ci zivotem?"
Hudebni Rozhledy, XIV, 22 (1961), 938.

1293. "Static on a hot tin roof." Time, LXXII (July 7,
1958), 58.

1294. Stauder, Wilhelm. Grenzen und Möglichkeiten elek-
troakustischer Hilfen in der Musik- und Sprach-
forschung. Frankfurt, University of Frankfurt,
1950.

1295. Steinecke, Wolfgang. "Aufführungen mit elektronischer Musik." Melos, XX (Jan. 1953), 17.

1296. Steinem, G. "Music, music, music, music." Show,
IV (Jan. 1964), 59.

1297. Steinhausen, H.-W. "Musische Technik." In Winckel,
ed., Klangstruktur der Musik. Berlin, Verlag
für Radio-Foto-Kinotechnik, 1955, 195.

1298. Steinke, Gerhard. "Experimental music with the

subharmonic sound apparatus 'Subharchord.'" Journal of the Audio Engineering Society, XIV, 2
(April 1966), 140.

1299. ------ "Experimentelle Musik I (1963/64)." Berlin,
Rundfunk- und Fernsehtechnisches Zentralamt der
Deutschen Post, 1964 (mimeograph).

1300. ------ "Über Vorarbeiten für ein Studio für künst-
liche Klang- und Geräuscherzeugung." Technische
Mitteilungen Rundfunk- und Fernsehtechnisches
Zentralamt, VIII, 4 (Dec. 1964), 168.

1301. Stephan, Rudolf. See Dahlhaus, Carl.

1302. Stockhausen, Karlheinz. "A proposito di musica
elettronica." Incontri musicale, 1 (1956), 70.
"Arbeitsbericht 1953: die Entstehung der elektronischen Musik." In Texte, Band 1. Köln,
Verlag M. DuMont Schauberg, 1963, 39.

1303. ------ "Aktuelles." Die Reihe, I (1955), 57.
In Texte, Band 2. Köln, Verlag M. DuMont Schauberg, 1964, 51. "Actualia." Die Reihe, 1 (1958),
45.

1304. ------ "Arbeitsbericht 1952/53: Orientierung."
Structure (Amsterdam), I (1958), 19. In Texte,
Band 1. Köln, Verlag M. DuMont Schauberg, 1963,
32.

1305. ------ "Chances de la musique électronique."
Phantomas, 15-16 (Jan. 1960). "Chancen der elek-
tronischen Musik." In Texte, Band 2. Köln,
Verlag M. DuMont Schauberg, 1964, 233.

1306. ------ "Die Einheit der musikalischen Zeit." In
Texte, Band 1. Köln, Verlag M. DuMont Schauberg,
1963, 211. Translated by Elaine Barkin as "The
concept of unity in electronic music." Perspectives of New Music, I, 1 (Fall 1962), 39.

1307. ------ "Electronic musical composition no. 2, 1953."
Ottawa, National Research Council of Canada, Technical Translation TT-611, 1956 (translation of 1314).

1308. ------ "Elektronische Musik und Automatik." Melos,
      XXXII, 10 (Oct. 1965), 337.

1309. ------ "Elektronische Studien I und II." In Texte,
      Band 2. Köln, Verlag M. DuMont Schauberg, 1964, 22

1310. ------ "Elektronische und instrumentale Musik."
      Die Reihe, V (1959), 50. In Texte, Band 1. Köln,
      Verlag M. DuMont Schauberg, 1963, 140. "Electronic
      and instrumental music." Die Reihe, 5 (1961), 59.

1311. ------ "Erfindung und Entdeckung." Neue Musik,
      (1961). In Texte, Band 1. Köln, Verlag M. DuMont
      Schauberg, 1963, 222. "Invention et découverte."
      In La musique et ses problèmes contemporaines 1953-
      1963. Paris, René Juilliard (Cahiers de la Com-
      pagnie Madeleine Renaud -- Jean-Louis Barrault,
      41), 1963, 147.

1312. ------ "Une expérience électronique." In La musique
      et ses problèmes contemporaines 1953-1963. Paris,
      René Juilliard, 1963, 91 (translation of 1314).

1313. ------ "Gesang der Jünglinge." In Texte, Band 2.
      Köln, Verlag M. DuMont Schauberg, 1964, 49.

1314. ------ "Komposition 1953 Nr. 2." Technische Haus-
      mitteilungen des Nordwestdeutschen Rundfunks, VI,
      1-2 (1954), 46. In Texte, Band 2. Köln, Verlag
      M. DuMont Schauberg, 1964, 23.

1315. ------ "Kontakte, für elektronische Klänge und zwei
      Instrumentalisten." In Texte, Band 2. Köln, Ver-
      lag M. DuMont Schauberg, 1964, 104.

1316. ------ "Mikrophonie I und Mikrophonie II." Melos,
      XXXIII, 11 (Nov. 1966), 354.

1317. ------ "Momentform." In Texte, Band 1. Köln, Ver-
      lag M. DuMont Schauberg, 1963, 189.

1318. ------ "Musik im Raum." Darmstädter Beiträge zur
      neuen Musik, II (1959), 30. Die Reihe, V (1959),
      59. In Texte, Band 1. Köln, Verlag M. DuMont
      Schauberg, 1963, 152. "Musique dans l'espace."
      Revue Belge de Musicologie, XIII, 1-4 (1959), 76.

"Music in space." Die Reihe, 5 (1961), 67.
"Musica nello spazio." La Rassegna musicale,
XXXI, 4 (1961), 397.

1319. ------ "Musik in Funktion." Melos, XXIV (1957),
249. In Die Stimme der Komponisten. Rodenkirchen/
Rhein, P.J. Tonger, 1958 (volume II of the series
Kontrapunkte, Heinrich Lindlar, ed.), 146. In
Texte, Band 2. Köln, Verlag M. DuMont Schauberg,
1963, 212. "Musique fonctionelle." In Avec Stravinsky. Monaco, 1958, 92.

1320. ------ "Musik kennt keine Grenzen." In Texte, Band
2. Köln, Verlag M. DuMont Schauberg, 1964, 210.

1321. ------ "Musik und Graphik." Darmstädter Beiträge
zur neuen Musik, III (1960). In Texte, Band 1.
Köln, Verlag M. DuMont Schauberg, 1963, 176.

1322. ------ "Musik und Sprache." Darmstädter Beiträge
zur neuen Musik, I (1958). Die Reihe, VI (1960),
36. "Music and speech." Die Reihe, 6 (1964), 40.

1323. ------ "Musikalische Eindrücke einer Amerikareise."
In Texte, Band 2. Köln, Verlag M. DuMont Schauberg, 1964, 219.

1324. ------ "Originale, musikalisches Theater." In
Texte, Band 2. Köln, Verlag M. DuMont Schauberg,
1964, 107.

1325. ------ "Originale: Partitur mit Erläuterungen."
In Texte, Band 2. Köln, Verlag M. DuMont Schauberg, 1964, 112.

1326. ------ "Situation actuelle du métier de composi-
teur." Domaine musicale, 1 (1954). "Zur situation des Metiers (Klangkomposition)." In Texte,
Band 1. Köln, Verlag M. DuMont Schauberg, 1963,
45.

1327. ------ "Studie II (Einführung der Partitur)."
In Texte, Band 2. Köln, Verlag M. DuMont Schauberg, 1964, 37.

1328. ------ Studie II. Reviewed in Neue Zeitschrift

für Musik, CXVIII (April 1957), 241.

1329. ------ Studie II. Reviewed in Notes, XVII (1960), 644.

1330. ------ Studie II. Reviewed in La Rassegna musicale, XXVII (Sept. 1957), 247.

1331. ------ Texte zur elektronischen und instrumentalen Musik (Band 1). Texte zu eigenen Werken, zur Kunst Anderer, Aktuelles (Band 2). Köln, Verlag M. DuMont Schauberg, 1963, 1964.

1332. ------ Texte. Reviewed in Neue Zeitschrift für Musik, CXXV, 11 (1964), 514.

1333. ------ "Vieldeutige Form." In Texte, Band 2. Köln, Verlag M. DuMont Schauberg, 1964, 245.

1334. ------ "Vorschläge" (Text für die Frankfurter Allgemeine Zeitung). In Texte, Band 2. Köln, Verlag M. DuMont Schauberg, 1964, 235. "Los kompozytora w świecie współczesnym." Ruch Muzyczny, VI, 15 (1962), 8.

1335. ------ " ... wie die Zeit vergeht ... " Die Reihe, III (1957), 13. In Texte, Band 1. Köln, Verlag M. DuMont Schauberg, 1963, 99. Translated by Cornelius Cardew as " ..... how time passes ..... " Die Reihe, 3 (1959), 10.

1336. ------ See Eimert, Herbert.

1337. "Stockhausen quoted on present music." Musical Courier, CLIX, 3 (Feb. 1959), 32.

1338. "Stockholmsstudion för elektronisk musik 1962." Dansk Musiktidsskrift, XXXIX, 4 (1964), 139.

1339. Stokowski, Leopold. "New horizons in music." Journal of the Acoustical Society of America, IV, 1 (July 1932), 11.

1340. Stone, Kurt. "Current chronicle: Lenox, Mass." The Musical Quarterly, LI, 4 (Oct. 1965), 688.

1341. ------ "Current chronicle: New York." The Musical
      Quarterly, XLIX, 3 (July 1963), 371.

1342. ------ "Reviews of records" (Columbia-Princeton
      composers). The Musical Quarterly, LII, 4 (Oct.
      1966), 538.

1343. ------ "Reviews of records" (Stockhausen: Gesang
      der Jünglinge, Kontakte). The Musical Quarterly,
      XLIX, 4 (Oct. 1963), 551.

1344. Strang, Gerald. "Computer music: analysis, synthe-
      sis, and composition" (abstract). Journal of the
      Acoustical Society of America, XXXIX, 6 (June
      1966), 1245.

1345. "Strange music!" American Record Guide, XXIII
      (March 1957), 88.

1346. "Stratford, Ontario: engineers lead composers."
      Musical America, LXXX (Oct. 1960), 33.

1347. Stravinsky, Igor and Robert Craft. "Electronic
      music." In Conversations with Igor Stravinsky.
      London, Faber and Faber, 1958, 111.

1348. ------ and ------ "Electronic music." In Memories
      and commentaries. Garden City, N.Y., Doubleday,
      1960, 94.

1349. Strobel, Heinrich. "Deutschland seit 1945."
      Melos, XXX (Dec. 1963), 404.

1350. Strongin, Theodore. "Ladies send out the 'far-
      out.'" The New York Times, CXIII (March 29,
      1964), section 2, 9.

1351. ------ "Oldtime avant-gardist." The New York Times,
      CXIV (Feb. 21, 1965), X13.

1352. Stuckenschmidt, Hans Heinz. "Contemporary tech-
      niques in music." The Musical Quarterly, XLIX, 1
      (Jan. 1963), 1.

1353. ------ "Die dritte Epoche"/"The third stage." Die
      Reihe, I/1 (1955/1958), 17/11.

1354. ------ "Entwicklung oder experiment." Darmstädter Beiträge zur neuen Musik, I (1958).

1355. ------ "Il mondo delle sonorità ignote: Un contributo all' estetica della musica elettronica." Aut Aut, 41 (July 1957), 399.

1356. ------ "Musical avant-garde gathers in Darmstadt for tenth year." Musical America, LXXVI (Sept. 1956), 6.

1357. ------ "Musik aud der Retorte." Theater der Zeit, I (1953), 16.

1358. ------ "Musik und Technik." In Winckel, ed., Klangstruktur der Musik. Berlin, Verlag für Radio-Foto-Kinotechnik, 1955, 209.

1359. ------ "Musique concrète." In Bericht über den Internationalen Musikwissenschaftlichen Kongress Kassel 1962. Kassel, Bärenreiter, 1963, 388.

1360. ------ "New world of electronic music evokes admiration and fear." Musical America, LXXVII (July 1957), 13.

1361. ------ Schöpfer der neuen Musik: Portraits und Studien. Frankfurt am Main, Suhrkamp, 1958.

1362. ------ Schöpfer der neuen Musik. Reviewed in Musica, XIII (May 1959), 342.

1363. "Studio voor elektronische muziek te Utrecht." Mens en Melodie, XVI (August 1961), 243.

1364. Suder, Alexander L. "Die überflüssige Windmaschine: eine Betrachtung zur 'elektronischen Musik.'" Zeitschrift für Musik, CXVI (August-Sept. 1955), 456.

1365. Suffield, Raymond. See Douglas, Alan.

1366. "Summary of recent use of musique concrète." World of Music, 3 (Jan. 1958), 11.

1367. Supper, Walter. "Zum elektronen-Instrument." Musik

und Altar, VI (1954), 199.

1368. Sursin, Albert. "La danse au Théâtre des Nations." Musica (Chaix), XCIX (June 1962), 36.

1369. Susa, Conrad S. "Music in our time." Musical America, LXXXIV, 2 (Feb. 1964), 41.

1370. Swickard, Ralph. "New electronic music laboratory at Yale U. dedicated." Music of the West Magazine, XVII (March 1962), 7.

1371. "Syncopation by automation." In Data from Electro-Data. Pasadena, California, Burroughs Corporation (ElectroData Division), August 1956, 2.

1372. Takatsuji, Tsukasa, Hisashi Fujita, Yoshinoir Ando, and Hiroshi Shiotani. "Electronic music" (in Japanese with English abstract). Technical Journal of the Japan Broadcasting Corporation, XIII, 4 (1961), 327.

1373. Tal, Josef. "Synthetic means." In Beckwith and Kasemets, eds., The modern composer and his world. Toronto, University of Toronto Press, 1961, 116.

1374. Tall, Joel. "Music without musicians." Saturday Review, XL (Jan. 26, 1957), 56.

1375. Tallmadge, W.H. "The composer's machine." Journal of Aesthetics and Art Criticism, XIX, 3 (1961), 339.

1376. Tamer, R.H. "Electronic music instruments -- past, present, and future" (abstract). Journal of the Acoustical Society of America, XXVI (1954), 931.

1377. Tardieu, Jean. "Décade de la musique expérimentale." La Revue musicale, 236 (1957), 103.

1378. Taubman, Howard. "Machines and men" (RCA synthesizer). The New York Times, CIV (Feb. 6, 1955), section 2, 9.

1379. Taylor, C.A. The physics of musical sounds. London, The English Universities Press, 1965, 179.

1380. Technische Hausmitteilungen des Nordwestdeutschen
      Rundfunks, VI, 1-2 (1954). Special issue devoted
      to electronic music (translated by National Re-
      search Council of Canada, Ottawa, 1956). Articles
      by Adams; Bode; Eimert; Eimert, Enkel, and Stock-
      hausen; Enkel; Enkel and Schütz; Meyer-Eppler;
      Stockhausen; and Trautwein.

1381. Teitelbaum, Richard. "Son-Nova 1988: electronic
      music by Bülent Arel, Mario Davidovsky, and
      Vladimir Ussachevsky" (review of recording).
      Perspectives of New Music, III, 1 (Fall-Winter
      1964), 127.

1382. Tennes, C.J. See Kent, Earle Lewis.

1383. Tenney, James. Meta (+) Hodos: a phenomenology of
      twentieth-century musical materials and an approach
      to the study of form. New Orleans, Tulane Univer-
      sity, 1964.

1384. ------ Meta (+) Hodos. Reviewed by John R. White
      in Current Musicology, (Spring 1966), 89.

1385. ------ "Musical composition with the computer"
      (abstract). Journal of the Acoustical Society
      of America, XXXIX, 6 (June 1966), 1245.

1386. ------ "Sound generation by means of a digital com-
      puter." Journal of Music Theory, VII, 1 (Spring
      1963), 24.

1387. "Théâtre Herbertot: première anthologie interna-
      tionale de musique concrète, électronique." Guide
      du concert, 409 (Dec. 14, 1963), 15.

1388. Thienhaus, Erich. "Die mechanisch-elektrischen
      Musikverfahren." In Fred Hamel and Martin Hürli-
      mann, eds., Das Atlantisbuch der Musik. Zürich,
      Atlantis Verlag, 1953, 821.

1389. ------ See Winckel, Fritz W.

1390. Thomas, Ernst. "Die junge Komponistengeneration
      in Darmstadt." Melos, XXVIII, 10 (Oct. 1961),
      322.

1391. ------ "Schreckenswort Hiroshima: Nonos Kantate und Eimerts Epitaph." Melos, XXX (March 1963), 91.

1392. Timmens, J. See Olson, Harry F.

1393. Tomkins, Calvin. "Profiles: John Cage -- figure in an imaginary landscape." The New Yorker, XL, 41 (Nov. 28, 1964), 64. Revised version in The bride and the bachelors. New York, Viking Press, 1965.

1394. Topel, H. "Probleme einer Analyse der Klangfarben-Modulation." Fernmelde Praxis, XXXIII (Nov. 1956), 817; XXXIV (March 1957), 195; (April 1957), 268; (May 1957), 348. Annales des Télécommunications, 91117 (March 1957); 94995 (July-August 1957); 97324 (Oct. 1957); 97325 (Oct. 1957).

1395. Trautwein, Friedrich. "The electronic monochord." Ottawa, National Research Council of Canada, Technical Translation TT-606, 1956 (translation of 1398).

1396. ------ Elektrische Musik. Berlin, Verlag Wiedmann, 1930.

1397. ------ "Elektroakustische Mittel in der aktiven Tonkunst." Acustica, IV, 1 (1954), 256.

1398. ------ "Das elektronische Monochord." Technische Hausmitteilungen des Nordwestdeutschen Rundfunks, VI, 1-2 (1954), 24.

1399. ------ "Das Klangfarben-Musikinstrument." Musica, VII (July-August 1953), 301.

1400. ------ "Toneinsatz und elektrische Musik." Zeitschrift für technische Physik, XIII (1932), 244.

1401. ------ "Über Imitation und Neuegestaltung in der elektronischen Musik." Instrumentenbau Zeitschrift, IX (1955), 181.

1402. ------ See Moles, Abraham André.

1403. Truding, Lona. "Musique concrète." Goethe, XXXIII 1954), 92.

1404. Truslit, A. "Kommt das Zeitalter der synthetischer Musik?" *Musica*, IV, 5-6 (May-June 1950), 176.

1405. Turok, Paul H. "The outrageous Stockhausen." *Music Journal*, XXII (Sept. 1964), 52.

1406. Ulbricht, H.W. "Akustische Artistik oder elektrische Musik?" *Zeitschrift für Musik*, CXIII (Feb. 1952), 69.

1407. Ulmann, H. von. "Elektronische Musik und Film." *Musica*, X, 12 (Dec. 1956), 867.

1408. Ulrich, Homer and Paul A. Pisk. *A history of music and musical style*. New York, Harcourt, Brace and World, Inc., 1963, 611, 658.

1409. Ulrich, P. "Neue Klänge setzen sich durch." *Musikhandel*, XIV (May 1963), 81.

1410. "Union card for a tape recorder." *Music Journal*, XXII (May 1954), 17.

1411. "University of Illinois; music and engineering students in a workshop." *Musical Courier*, CLIX, 4 (March 1959), 41.

1412. "Urges copyright protection for new electronic music." *Billboard*, (August 25, 1958), 4.

1413. "U.S. elementary schools enjoying 'Poem in cycles and bells,' Luening-Ussachevsky." *Bulletin of American Composers Alliance*, IX, 4 (1961), 10.

1414. "USA: 'Avantgardistische' Musik." *Musik und Gesellschaft*, XIV (May 1964), 319.

1415. "The use of the computer in music and musicology: draft bibliography (unified)." New York, New York University Institute for Computer Research in the Humanities, undated (mimeograph).

1416. Ussachevsky, Vladimir A. "As Europe takes to tape." *Bulletin of American Composers Alliance*, III, 3 (1953), 10.

1417. ------ "Columbia-Princeton electronic music center."
Revue Belge de Musicologie, XIII, 1-4 (1959), 129.

1418. ------ "Music in the tape medium." Juilliard Review, VI (Spring 1959), 8.

1419. ------ "Musical timbre by means of the Klangumwandler." Audio Engineering Society Preprint No. 65,
1958.

1420. ------ "Notes on A piece for tape recorder." The
Musical Quarterly, XLVI, 2 (April 1960), 202. In
Lang, ed., Problems of modern music. New York,
W.W. Norton, 1962, 64.

1421. ------ "The processes of experimental music."
Journal of the Audio Engineering Society, VI, 3
(July 1958), 202.

1422. ------ "Some of the specialized equipment developed
in electronic music studios." Paper read at the
session "Music and Electronics," Audio Engineering
Society, Oct. 5-9, 1959.

1423. ------ "Sound materials in the experimental media
of musique concrète, tape music, and electronic
music." (abstract). Journal of the Acoustical
Society of America, XXIX (1957), 768.

1424. ------ "La 'tape music' aux États-Unis." La Revue
musicale, 236 (1957), 50.

1425. ------ "Synthetic means." In Beckwith and Kasemets,
eds., The modern composer and his world. Toronto,
University of Toronto Press, 1961, 121.

1426. ------ See Carter, Elliott. See Moles, Abraham
André.

1427. "Ussachevsky in his NYC laboratory, Otto Luening
with his instrument." Musical Courier, LXI (June
1961), 17.

1428. "Utrecht" (Review of Mauricio Kagel's "Sur scène").
Mens en Melodie, XVIII (Dec. 1963), 376.

1429. Vandel Heuvel, Jean. "The fantastic sounds of LaMonte Young." Vogue, CXLVII, 9 (May 1966), 198.

1430. Vandelle, Romuald. "Mémoire et musique." Situation de la recherche, Cahiers d'études de radio-télévision, 27-28 (Sept.-Dec. 1960), 240. Paris, Flammarion.

1431. ------ "Musique exotique et musique expérimentale." La Revue musicale, 244 (1959), 34.

1432. Vander Linden, Albert. "Belgium from 1914 to 1964." In Lang and Broder, eds., Contemporary music in Europe. New York, G. Schirmer, 1965, 92. The Musical Quarterly, LI, 1 (Jan. 1965), 92.

1433. Varèse, Edgar. "Answers." Possibilities, (Winter 1947-1948), 96.

1434. ------ "A communication." The Musical Quarterly, XLI (1955), 574.

1435. ------ "Erinnerungen und Gedanken." Darmstädter Beiträge zur neuen Musik, III (1960), 65.

1436. ------ "Les instruments de musique et la machine électronique." L'Age nouveau, 92 (May 1955), 28.

1437. ------ "Musik auf neuen Wegen." Stimmen, XV (1949), 401.

1438. ------ "Organized sound for the sound film." Commonweal, XXXIII (1940), 204.

1439. ------ See Schuller, Gunther.

1440. ------ et al. "Discussion" (of synthetic means). In Beckwith and Kasemets, eds., The modern composer and his world. Toronto, University of Toronto Press, 1961, 126.

1441. Vega, Aurelio de la. "Electronic music, tool of creativity." Music Journal, XXIII (Sept. 1965), 52; (Oct. 1965), 61; (Nov. 1965), 52.

1442. ------ "Regarding electronic music." Tempo, 75

(Winter 1965-1966), 2.

1443. "Venice report: congress for experimental music."
World of Music, III, 3 (June 1961), 66.

1444. Verken, Monique. "Petite introduction à la musique
électronique." Cahiers musicaux, 12 (March 1957).

1445. Vermeulen, R. "Musik und Elektroakustik"/"Music
and electroacoustics." Gravesaner Blätter/Grave-
sano Review, V, 17 (1960), 2/7.

1446. ------ "Stereo-Nachhall." Philips Technical Review,
XVII, 9 (Jan. 1956), 258.

1447. Vlad, Roman. "Die Reihe and electronic music."
Score, 13 (Sept. 1955), 23.

1448. ------ "Le nuove vie della giovane musica" (Darmstadt, 1961). La Rassegna musicale, XXXI, 4
(1961), 343.

1449. ------ "La serialità integrale e la musica elettronica." In Storia della dodecafonia. Milano,
Suivini Zerboni, 1958.

1450. Voss, Robert M. "The Brandeis University electronic
music studio." Journal of the Audio Engineering
Society, XIII, 1 (Jan. 1965), 65. Discussion,
XIII, 2 (April 1965), 183.

1451. Waldmann, G. "Elektronische Musik in Trossingen."
Das Musikleben, VI (March 1953), 100.

1452. Wallner, Bo. "Scandinavian music after the Second
World War." In Lang and Broder, eds., Contemporary music in Europe. New York, G. Schirmer,
1965, 111. The Musical Quarterly, LI, 1 (Jan.
1965), 111.

1453. Walter, Arnold. "Music and electronics." Canadian
Music Journal, III, 4 (Summer 1959), 33.

1454. Walter, Jacob. "Mechanische Musik." Melos, XVII
(1950), 65.

1455. Walter, Nikolaus. "Gotteslob mit Radio-Röhren."
      Musik und Kirche, XXIII (1955), 101.

1456. Wangermée, Robert. "Contemporary music in America."
      Inter-American Music Bulletin, 22 (March 1961),
      12.

1457. Ward, Robert. "New electronic media." Juilliard
      Review, V (Spring 1958), 17.

1458. "Warsaw: international festival of contemporary
      music -- comments on David Tudor performing."
      The Music Review, XIX, 4 (Nov. 1958), 334.

1459. Warschauer, F. "Elektrische Tonerzeugung." An-
      bruch, IX, 5 (1929).

1460. Waterhouse, J.C. "The Italian avant-garde and
      national tradition." Tempo, 68 (Spring 1964), 14.

1461. Watson, R.B. "Composer's music box: electro-acous-
      tical tone generator." Journal of the Acoustical
      Society of America, XXI (May 1949), 214.

1462. Wayne, William C. "Electronic production of choral
      tone" (abstract). Journal of the Acoustical Soci-
      ety of America, XXXI (1959), 839.

1463. Weaver, Warren. See Shannon, C.E.

1464. Weisse, Karlhans. See Scerri, A.

1465. Weissmann, John S. "Current chronicle: Italy."
      The Musical Quarterly, L, 2 (April 1964), 243.

1466. ------ See Wörner, Karl H.

1467. "Welturaufführung der ersten elektronischen Messe."
      Gottesdienst und Kirchenmusik, 4 (1964), 161.

1468. "Wer ist Iannis Xenakis?"/"Who is Iannis Xenakis?"
      Gravesaner Blätter/Gravesano Review, VI, 23-24
      (1962), 185/186.

1469. "Werner Meyer-Eppler" (obituary). Gravesaner Blät-
      ter/Gravesano Review, V, 19-20 (1960), 2/3.

1470. White, John R. See Tenney, James.

1471. White, S.J. Letter. High Fidelity, VII, 1 (Jan.
      1957), 15.

1472. ------ Letter (reply to 1205). Saturday Review,
      XLVII (Nov. 28, 1964), 66.

1473. Whiteford, Joseph E. "Electronic reverberation."
      The American Organist, XLIV, 9 (Sept. 1961), 11.

1474. Whitney, John. "Bewegungsbilder und elektronische
      Musik"/"Moving pictures and electronic music."
      Die Reihe, VII/7 (1960/1965), 62/61.

1475. Whittenberg, Charles. "Ussachevsky's film music."
      Bulletin of American Composers Alliance, XI, 1
      (1963), 5.

1476. Wijdeveld, Wolfgang. "Een compositie voor elektron-
      ische klanksporen en orgel van Ton Bruynèl (Reliëf
      1964)." Mens en Melodie, XX (April 1965), 111.
      Appears in English and German as "Ton Bruynèl: Re-
      lief 1964." Sonorum Speculum, 25 (Winter 1965), 29.

1477. Wilding-White, Raymond and William Hemsath. "Sta-
      tus of the Case Studio for Experimental Music."
      Cleveland, Case Institute of Technology Studio
      for Experimental Music, Technical Report No. 2,
      1965 (mimeograph).

1478. Wilkinson, Marc. "An introduction to the music of
      Edgar Varèse." Score, 19 (March 1957), 5.

1479. ------ "Two months in the 'Studio di Fonologia.'"
      Score, 22 (Feb. 1958), 41.

1480. Wilks, J. "Dartington course in electronic music."
      Score, 28 (Jan. 1961), 71.

1481. "Will a machine compose a new symphony?" The
      School Musician, XXXI, 5 (Jan. 1960), 59.

1482. Winckel, Fritz W. "Berliner Elektronik." Melos,
      XXX, 9 (Sept. 1963), 279.

1483. ------ "Computermusik." Musica, XIX, 1 (1965), 45.

1484. ------ "Elektrische Musikinstrumente." In Die Musik in Geschichte und Gegenwart, III. Kassel, Bärenreiter, 1954, 1254.

1485. ------ "Fortschritte der Elektroakustik." Musica, VIII (Nov. 1954), 510.

1486. ------ "Gedanken zum Ton-Form-Problem." Film und Bild, Zeitschrift der Reichsanstalt für Film und Bild in Wissenschaft und Unterricht, 6 (1941).

1487. ------ "Die Grenzen der musikalischen Perzeption unter besonderer Berücksichtigung der elektronischen Musik." Archiv für Musikwissenschaft, XV, 4 (1958), 307.

1488. ------ "Hochschule-Universal-Mischpult für Experimentierzwecke." Elektronische Rundschau, VII (1959), 247.

1489. ------ "Die informationstheoretische Analyse musikalischer Strukturen." Die Musikforschung, XVII, 1 (1964), 1.

1490. ------ "Informationstheoretische Betrachtungen über Gehor und Hörgeräte." In Schubert, ed., Theorie und Praxis der Hörgeräteampassung, sowie Probleme Begutachtung. Stuttgart, Georg Thieme Verlag, 1960.

1491. ------ Klangwelt unter der Lupe. Berlin-Halensee, Max Hesses Verlag, 1952.

1492. ------ Klangwelt unter der Lupe. Reviewed by Arnold M. Small in Journal of the Acoustical Society of America, XXV, 4 (1953), 802.

1493. ------ "Komposition durch Phonomontage." Musica, IX (Dec. 1955), 601.

1494. ------ "Die Komposition mit elektroakustischen Mitteln." Neue Zeitschrift für Musik, CXX (March 1959), 124.

1495. ------ "Komposition mit elektronischen Klängen." Musica, XII (Dec. 1958), 769.

1496. ------ "Die Lautsynthese in der elektronischen
Musik." Physikalische Blätter, XVIII, 4 (1962),
153.

1497. ------ "Der Laut-Synthetisator nach Olson." Elektronische Rundschau, X, 8 (August 1956), 219.
Annales des Télécommunications, 88524 (Dec. 1956).

1498. ------ "Limites de la musique électronique." Revue
Belge de Musicologie, XIII, 1-4 (1959), 26. "Li-
miti fisio-acustici della musica elettronica." La
Rassegna musicale, XXXI, 4 (1961), 466.

1499. ------ "Naturwissenschaftliche Probleme der Musik."
Humanismus und Technik, II, 1 (1954), 12. In
Winckel, ed., Klangstruktur der Musik. Berlin,
Verlag für Radio-Foto-Kinotechnik, 1955, 11.

1500. ------ "Neues Hören in eignen Heim." Melos, XXVI
(1959), 201.

1501. ------ Phänomene des musikalischen Hörens. Berlin-
Halensee, Max Hesses Verlag, 1960.

1502. ------ "The psycho-acoustical analysis of structure
as applied to electronic music." Journal of Music
Theory, VII, 2 (1963), 194.

1503. ------ "Die psychophysischen Bedingungen des Musik-
hörens." In Stilkriterien der neuen Musik. Berlin,
Verlag Merseburger, 1961, 44.

1504. ------ "Von den Wandlungen des Klangstils: über das
Farbspektrum der Musik." Melos, XIX (1952), 135.

1505. ------ "Von der leichten zur 'leichtesten' Musik."
Gravesaner Blätter, 2-3 (Jan. 1956), 46.

1506. ------ Vues nouvelles sur le monde des sons. Paris,
Dunod, 1960 (translation of 1491).

1507. ------ "25 Jahre elektronische Musik." Musica, VI
(1952), 285.

1508. ------ ed. Klangstruktur der Musik. Berlin, Verlag
für Radio-Foto-Kinotechnik, 1955.

1509. ------ ed. Klangstruktur der Musik. Reviewed by
E. Thienhaus in Journal of the Acoustical Society
of America, XXIX (1957), 398.

1510. ------ ed. Klangstruktur der Musik. Reviewed in
Melos, XXIII (May 1956), 138.

1511. ------ ed. Klangstruktur der Musik. Reviewed in
Musik und Kirche, XXVI (May-June 1956), 129.

1512. ------ ed. Klangstruktur der Musik. Reviewed in
Die Musikforschung, IX, 4 (1956), 496.

1513. Windmuller, H.J. "Der Anteil des Kölner Studios
an der Entwicklung der elektronischen Musik."
Köln (?), unpublished manuscript.

1514. Wiora, Walter. Die vier Weltalter der Musik. Stuttgart, W. Kohlhammer, 1961, 156. Translated by J.
Gaudefrois-Demomdynes as Les quatre âges de la
musique. Paris, Petite Bibliothèque Payot, undated, 193. Translated by M.D. Herter Norton as
The four ages of music. New York, W.W. Norton,
1965, 182.

1515. Wismeyer, L. "Wider die Natur!" Neue Zeitschrift
für Musik, CXVIII (Feb. 1957), 136.

1516. Wolf, Arthur W. "Shostakovich on lack of Russian
interest in electronic music." Musical Courier,
CLXI, 1 (Jan. 1960), 23.

1517. Wolf, Werner. "Die Entwicklung und Verwendung
elektro-akustischer Musikinstrumente." Musik und
Gesellschaft, IV (1954), 445.

1518. Wolff, Christian. "New and electronic music."
Audience, V, 3 (Summer 1958).

1519. Woodworth, George Wallace. The world of music.
Cambridge, Mass., Belknap Press of Harvard University Press, 1964, 98.

1520. Wörner, Karl H. Karlheinz Stockhausen: Werk + Wol-
len 1950-1962. Rodenkirchen/Rhein, P.J. Tonger,
1963 (volume VI of the series Kontrapunkte, Hein-

rich Lindlar, ed.).

1521. ------ <u>Karlheinz Stockhausen</u>. Reviewed by John S. Weissmann in <u>Tempo</u>, 70 (Autumn 1964), 32.

1522. ------ "Die Klangwelt der elektronischen Musik." In <u>Neue Musik in der Entscheidung</u>. Mainz, Schott, 1954, 296.

1523. ------ "Musik und Technik." <u>Das Musikleben</u>, VII (1954), 241.

1524. ------ "Neue Musik 1948/58." <u>Darmstädter Beiträge zur neuen Musik</u>, II (1959).

1525. Wouters, Jos. "Holländische Musik im zwanzigsten Jahrhundert." <u>Oesterreichische Musikzeitschrift</u>, XIX (July 1964), 309. "Dutch music in the 20th century." In Lang and Broder, eds., <u>Contemporary music in Europe</u>. New York, G. Schirmer, 1965, 97. <u>The Musical Quarterly</u>, LI, 1 (Jan. 1965), 97.

1526. Wright, Howard. See Zaripov, R.Kh.

1527. Wright, W.V. See Brooks, F.P., Jr.

1528. Wrisch, Gerhard F. "Oskar Sala und das Mixtur-Trautonium." <u>Musikblätter</u>, X (1956), 101.

1529. "Write your own music with this new machine." <u>The Financial Post</u> (Toronto), I, 39 (Sept. 29, 1956), 52.

1530. "Writing music with electrons." <u>Radio-TV Experimenter</u>, (August-Sept. 1965), 70.

1531. Wuorinen, Charles. "The outlook for young composers." <u>Perspectives of New Music</u>, I, 2 (Spring 1963), 54.

1532. "Wykaz kompozycji zrealizowanych w Studio eksperymentalnym." <u>Ruch Muzyczny</u>, VII, 1 (1963), 6.

1533. Wylie, Ruth. "Musimatics: a view from the mainland." <u>Journal of Aesthetics and Art Criticism</u>, XXIV, 2 (Winter 1965), 287.

1534. Xenakis, Yannis. "Auf der Suche nach einer Stochastischen Musik"/"In search of a stochastic music."
Gravesaner Blätter/Gravesano Review, III, 11-12
(1958), 98/112.

1535. ------ "Un cas; la musique stochastique." Musica
(Chaix), 102 (Sept. 1962), 11.

1536. ------ "Le Corbusier's 'Elektronisches Gedicht'"/
"Corbusier's 'Electronic poem.'" Gravesaner Blät-
ter/Gravesano Review, III, 9 (1957), 43/51.

1537. ------ "Freie stochastische Musik durch den Elek-
tronenrechner"/"Free stochastic music from the
computer." Gravesaner Blätter/Gravesano Review,
VII, 26 (1965), 54/79.

1538. ------ "Grundlagen einer stochastischen Musik"/
"Elements of stochastic music." Gravesaner Blät-
ter/Gravesano Review, V, 18 (1960) 61/84; V, 19-
20 (1960), 128/140; VI, 21 (1961), 102/113; VI,
22 (1961), 131/144.

1539. ------ "Musiques formelles: nouveaux principes
formels de composition musicale." La Revue musicale, 253-254 (1963). Appears also as Musiques
formelles. Paris, Éditions Richard-Masse, 1963.

1540. ------ "Muzyka stochastyczna (swobona)." Ruch
Muzyczny, VII, 6 (1963), 1.

1541. ------ "Notes sur un 'geste électronique.'" Nutida
Musik (Stockholm), I (March 1958). La Revue musicale, 244 (1959), 25.

1542. ------ "Pierre Schaeffer." In Die Musik in Geschichte und Gegenwart, XI. Kassel, Bärenreiter,
1963, 1535.

1543. ------ "Stochastische Musik"/"Stochastic music."
Gravesaner Blätter/Gravesano Review, VI, 23-24
(1962), 156/169.

1544. ------ "Les trois paraboles." Nutida Musik (Stockholm), II (1958-1959).

1545. ------ "Wahrscheinlichkeitstheorie und Musik."
      Gravesaner Blätter, 6 (Dec. 1956), 28.

1546. ------ See Jeanneret-Gris, Charles-Édouard.

1547. "Xenakis: un jeune architecte grec." Guide du
      concert, 357 (June 8, 1962), 1456.

1548. Yates, Peter B. "John Cage: builder of new music."
      Vogue, CXLIV (Oct. 1, 1964), 225.

1549. ------ "Music: a long round trip -- 3." Arts and
      Architecture, LXXX, 6 (June 1963) 8.

1550. ------ "Music: correspondence" (letter from Gordon
      Mumma). Arts and Architecture, LXXXIII, 2 (Feb.-
      March 1966), 45.

1551. ------ "Music: musical computers at Urbana." Arts
      and Architecture, LXXXII, 6 (June 1965), 8.

1552. Young, LaMonte and Jackson MacLow. An anthology.
      New York, Young and MacLow, 1963.

1553. Zaripov, Rudolf Khafizovich. Kibernetica i muzyka.
      Moskva, Izd-vo Znanie, 1963.

1554. ------ "On algorithmic expression of musical compo-
      sitions." Doklady (Akademiya Nauk, USSR), CXXXII,
      6 (1960), 1283.

1555. ------ "On an algorithmic description of the process
      involved in the composition of music (ARTINT)."
      Automation Express, III, 3 (Nov. 1960), 17.

1556. ------ "On an algorithmic description ... ." Re-
      viewed by Howard Wright in Journal of the Associa-
      tion for Computing Machinery, 6124 0893.

1557. ------ "Programming the process of music composi-
      tion." Problemy Kibernetiki, VII (1962), 151.

1558. Zielinski, T.A. "Avantgardistische ensembles in
      Krakau und Warschau." Melos, XXXI (May 1964),
      168.

1559. ------ "Genealogia nowej muzyki." <u>Ruch Muzyczny</u>,
      VII, 20 (1963), 3; 21 (1963), 12.

1560. Zimin, P. "Vnimanie elektroinstrumentam." <u>Sovet-</u>
      <u>skaya Muzyka</u>, XXIII (Oct. 1959), 137.

1561. Zupko, Ramon. "Darmstadt: new directions." <u>Per-</u>
      <u>spectives of New Music</u>, II, 2 (Spring-Summer 1964),
      166.

1562. "Zürich." <u>Schweizerische Musikzeitung</u>, XCVII (May
      1957), 191.

1563. "Zwischen Elektronik und Elektronium." <u>Musica</u>, IX
      (July 1955), 350.

Aesthetics and criticism.
9ff, 15, 17, 27, 30, 57,
129, 154, 178, 342, 344,
349f, 353ff, 423, 453,
477, 511, 543, 677, 693,
695f, 710f, 727, 792,
836ff, 842, 880, 909,
981f, 991, 1059, 1076f,
1090, 1127, 1142, 1188,
1198, 1205, 1249, 1255,
1331, 1347f, 1353, 1355,
1498f, 1514, 1516, 1533.

Algorithmic processes.
69ff, 775f, 896, 1086,
1553ff.

Amplitude suppression or
"filtering." 745, 1051.

Arel, Bülent. 822.

Babbitt, Milton. 434, 464.

Badings, Henk. 1291, 1525.

Berio, Luciano. 540, 765.

Bibliography. 46, 77, 109,
282, 364, 371, 542, 699,
810, 1111, 1415, 1477.

Boulez, Pierre. 185, 208,
960, 1236.

Cage, John. 185, 188, 191,
208, 407, 409, 489, 512,
591, 712, 833, 1277,
1296, 1393, 1548.

Cahill, Thaddeus. 34, 63,
179, 450.

Computers. 145, 440ff,
447, 486, 561, 565ff,
590, 653, 726, 779,
925, 929, 995, 1018f,
1022, 1025, 1094, 1101,
1121, 1162, 1252, 1371,
1483.
Computer composition.
64, 168, 295, 419, 456,
513, 563f, 571, 944,
975, 1240, 1556.
Computer sound genera-
tion. 217, 238f, 416,
553, 750, 811ff, 1386.

Copyrights. 120, 246,
1412.

Dance, applications to.
60, 67, 412, 591, 672,
681, 749, 1160, 1368.

Discography. 277, 1111,
1133.

Dockstader, Tod. 268.

Duration and frequency
regulation. 800, 1283ff.

Education, use in.
546, 638, 705, 1413.

Electronic musical instruments (general). 257,
298, 302ff, 371, 376,

670, 685ff, 692, 701,
729, 763, 862, 919,
1003, 1115ff, 1208,
1227f, 1276, 1298f,
1367, 1484, 1517.

Enkel, Fritz. 437.

Films, use in. 75, 183,
476, 740, 753, 863,
1171, 1407, 1438, 1474.

Filters; formants. 5f,
868, 914.

Generators (specialized).
84, 335, 1461. See
Klangumwandler.

Grainger, Percy. 465.

Hamograph. 111, 1168.

Hand-drawn sound. 639,
644, 740, 985, 1015,
1529.

Heiss, Hermann. 379, 733,
736.

Henry, Pierre. 93, 421,
1265, 1368.

History. 716, 772, 899,
1070, 1078, 1524.
  Before 1948. 46, 63,
  73, 114, 179, 184, 186,
  209, 448, 450, 459,
  466f, 747, 789, 799,
  871, 1140, 1207, 1215,
  1339, 1396, 1400,
  1433, 1438, 1459.
  Computer music. 547ff,
  567.
  Elektronische Musik.
  112f, 115f, 338ff, 350,

377, 1507, 1513, 1522.
Musique concrète. 37,
  74, 76, 249, 573f, 754,
  934, 936f, 1092, 1134,
  1172, 1184, 1189, 1198,
  1247.
Tape music. 190, 252,
  1417, 1424.

Information theory. 33,
211, 220, 440ff, 523,
551f, 606, 847, 849f,
892f, 902, 906, 909,
1020, 1023, 1028, 1089,
1097, 1251, 1489f.

Jacobs, Henry. 431.

Klangumwandler (single-
sideband generator).
139, 520, 1419.

Luening, Otto C. 91, 774,
960, 1413, 1427.

Melochord; Monochord.
135f, 1395, 1398.

Meyer-Eppler, Werner. 348,
1469.

Musical space. 96, 1011,
1318.

Musical time. 54, 96,
1178, 1206, 1306, 1335.

Nilsson, Bo. 657.

Notation. 142, 356f, 517,
659, 848, 911, 1060,
1327f.

Philippot, Michel. 398.

RCA Synthesizer. 51, 195,

374, 449, 579f, 703, 946f, 965, 967ff, 1375, 1378, 1496f.

Die Reihe. 58, 279, 1447.

Religion, applications to. 379, 655, 736, 1467.

Reverberation. 1229, 1446, 1473.

Reviews of recordings. 29, 224, 226f, 276, 359, 418, 428ff, 521, 560, 584, 603, 1152, 1156, 1158, 1342f, 1381.

Schaeffer, Pierre. 611, 971, 1542.

Serial techniques. 17, 55, 485, 953, 1048f, 1142, 1167, 1449.

Stereophony. 95, 174, 248, 664, 1007, 1098.

Stochastic processes. 44, 1534f, 1537ff, 1543ff.

Stockhausen, Karlheinz. 110, 164, 182, 630, 752, 769, 1203, 1206, 1213f, 1263, 1405, 1520f.

Studio techniques. 390, 394, 396, 661f, 846, 1040f, 1147, 1420f.

Studios. 1111.
Belgium. 369, 1432.
Brandeis University. 1450.
Case Institute. 1477.
Chile. 218.

Columbia-Princeton. 234, 700, 970, 986, 1009, 1032, 1113, 1417. See History: tape music. See RCA Synthesizer.
Czechoslovakia. 631f, 1163.
England. 622, 1037.
Gravesano. 405, 483, 492, 600, 757, 910, 1103f, 1164, 1245.
Helsinki. 537.
Illinois. 360, 549, 554, 1411, 1551.
Independent. 920.
Italy. 104f, 202, 382, 604, 744, 746, 942, 951, 1063, 1272, 1479.
Japan. 292, 916, 1372.
Köln. 389, 391, 425, 751, 839. See History: elektronische Musik.
The Netherlands. 59, 281, 724, 1525.
Paris. See History: musique concrète.
Stockholm. 1338, 1452.
Toronto. 111, 365, 605, 1166, 1530.
USSR. 28, 278, 919, 924, 1061, 1553f.
Warsaw. 607, 939, 987f, 1034, 1136, 1532.
Yale University. 705, 1125, 1370.

Tal, Josef. 480, 614, 1119.

Tape devices (specialized). 526, 718, 720, 1165.

Terminology. 860, 864, 1004.

The "Tonmeister." 4, 166.

Touch-sensitive keying
devices. 721f, 872.

Trautwein, Friedrich; Trautonium. 147, 280, 452,
1145ff, 1528.

Tudor, David. 188f, 712,
1458. See Cage, John.

Union (American Federation
of Musicians). 587, 756,
1006.

Ussachevsky, Vladimir A.

251, 297, 728, 774, 960,
1159, 1278, 1413, 1427,
1475.

Varèse, Edgar. 193, 214,
491, 608f, 665, 1057,
1219, 1232, 1478, 1536.

Voltage controlled devices.
84, 913f.

Wuorinen, Charles. 213.

Xenakis, Yannis. 1268,
1468, 1547.